What's Your Price

THE ONLINE DATING AUCTION

Adam Gilad

WHAT'S YOUR PRICE

The Online Dating Auction

InfoStream Group Inc.
Copyright© 2012

ISBN-13: 978-0991008919
LOC#: 2012951911

Published by Ivy Street Press
6871 S. Eastern Avenue Ste. 101
Las Vegas, NV 89119
www.InfoStreamGroup.com

Printed in the United   States of America

CONTENTS

PREFACE

Some of you may have heard of my story by now. You may have seen me on television, be it on 20/20, Dr. Phil, Anderson Cooper, or Dr. Drew, defending my dating websites. You may have been curious and you may have paid my sites a visit. Some of you were probably intrigued and some of you offended, possibly because you feel excluded. Some of you may have taken the plunge by joining one of my dating websites in search of what may be missing in your life—be it something deep such as love, companionship, friendship, intimacy, or something more shallow, like sex or money.

No matter what you seek, as humans, we are driven to take action—to do *something*—because we either want to avoid pain or seek pleasure. The pain I suffered from being shy with women and as a result having to face loneliness up until I was 21 years old, when I had my first kiss, has lingered with me until now. But once I experienced that first kiss, the pleasure I had been missing was unleashed upon me, and became the driver of my quest to find romance, love, and intimacy.

Over the years, I have tried numerous approaches at dating. I joined a traditional dating agency. I participated in speed-dating events. I parted with my hard-earned money on It's Just Lunch. I even joined a host of dating websites, including Match.com and eHarmony. None of these methods worked for me. Why? Because the initial stages of dating are a dance influenced by superficial attributes such as first impressions, charisma, six-pack abs, huge biceps, or big boobs. As a nerd who was shy and who had shunned the gym, I stood no chance in this mating game.

It was my mother's advice to me growing up, telling me to focus on my grades. She said, "Once you are successful and you have the financial means, the dating game will change in your favor." Those words ultimately led me to create numerous online dating options. I started with SeekingArrangement.com, a dating website where beautiful women outnumber generous men ten to one. This was followed by WhatsYourPrice.com, the subject of this book, where the generous can bid for a first date with the attractive. And more recently, I created MissTravel.com, a travel dating website where the generous can find attractive travel companions.

The motivations behind all of my dating websites, and more specifically WhatsYourPrice.com, are clear. If I didn't have the means to compete superficially with amazing good looks, physique, or pick-up skills, perhaps I can compete superficially—with *generosity*. Generosity and wealth, just like biceps, can land me a first date, giving you or anyone like me the chance to compete on a level playing field.

Many people ask me if I believe that money can buy love. I don't. Money can't buy love, just like amazing good looks or physique can't guarantee love. But money and generosity, just like good looks or physique, can help to improve your chances at finding love. And that is the premise behind WhatsYourPrice.com.

Does WhatsYourPrice.com work? I believe so. And can it really be used to find love and romance? I am sure it can. Over the past year, hundreds of members have reached out to me to tell me of their successes. I heard from men. I have also heard from amazingly beautiful women like Jane, a beautiful model from California, who told me she met her current boyfriend on the website. Even though he wasn't the type she normally dates, through WhatsYourPrice.com she decided to give him a chance by going on that first date, and the rest is history.

WhatsYourPrice.com is a winning dating system for average guys. And while you may have heard that "nice guys finish last", nice guys who use the website correctly always end up winning. The truth is, women are superficially attracted to bad boys because they seem so cool on the outside, but if given the chance to get to know a nice guy who is ready to pamper and spoil, no woman in her right mind will choose a bad boy over a nice one. Testimonials on WhatsYourPrice.com feature countless numbers of gorgeous women, grateful they had the chance to meet that genuinely nice guy.

And while I have received a great deal of positive feedback, I have also received just as many complaints.

One major complaint I hear often is how some attractive members are gaming the system, uploading fake photos or very old photos of themselves, then showing up at dates looking like nothing on their profile. While we have stated in our FAQ that generous members are not obligated to pay if the person showing up does not look the same as their profile photo, many generous members are too nice to simply walk away. (This isn't just a problem on our website; it is far worse on other—virtually unregulated—dating sites.) To solve this problem, I have invented a patent-pending photo verification system that is currently in development. I hope that soon after this book is published, the inaccurate photo problem will be a thing of the past on my sites.

But the complaints aren't just from the generous members. Attractive members have told me of generous members trying to game the system by making an offer, going out on a date, and then refusing to honor their agreement to pay for the date. While I do not expect these "bad boys" to be too successful in using the website, I am currently working on a non-intrusive rating system intended to discourage this type of behavior. In the near future, rule-abiding members who are receiving good ratings will have a trustworthy star attached to their profiles.

As more and more people meet online, it is important that we raise awareness to the dangers of online dating. While I have urged many of the users of my dating websites to be careful and to use common sense, still, many members are overly trusting. Many of these trusting members have been known to send money to a stranger with a sob story, or to fly out to meet a stranger only to be stranded in the airport. So in addition to providing our members with sufficient warnings, my goal is to make online dating on our websites even safer. We will soon be adding a background and criminal verification option to WhatsYourPrice.com.

I realize WhatsYourPrice.com isn't exactly a perfect dating system yet. There are still some major flaws, but I am working hard to fix those. I am a strong believer in innovation, and I also believe nothing is impossible. So over the upcoming months and years, I will continue to invent new solutions to level the dating playing field at WhatsYourPrice.com.

When I met Adam Gilad over a year ago, he was already a very successful dating coach and coach. While many of the relationship experts, dating coaches, and some in the pick-up community have scoffed at the idea of WhatsYourPrice.com, Adam was open-minded enough to accept my invitation to take a closer look at the website and see what it was doing for its members.

This book is the result of Adam's research with many of our members.

He, like most successful people, understands that there can be no reward without risk, and this holds true especially in love. Some of you may have picked up this book in an effort to find the pleasure of romance or companionship. Some of you, like me, may be searching for a solution to the pain of loneliness or shyness. But whatever the reasons may be, I applaud you for taking action, and wish you the best in your journey. I hope my creation will play its part in helping you find excitement and everlasting happiness.

Brandon Wade
Founder & CEO
WhatsYourPrice.com

Los Angeles, California
September 19, 2012

AUTHOR'S PREFACE

In 2001, after 17 years of marriage, I found myself—at age 39, father of two and hyper-educated—single. I had married young, plucking a beautiful young thing, full of hope and talent, from a pathologically negative family. And with all the naïveté of youth, I thought I could blossom her into joy.

I couldn't.

Seventeen years later, I found myself on the dating market, utterly unequipped. I had never flirted. I had resisted temptation when those cute little Korean freshman girls used to come in for my writing and poetry class office hours at Stanford University, clearly enamored by the first man they had ever met who passionately encouraged self-expression over yet another A+ or competition win. I had never been to a bar, a club, or dated as an adult.

But when I discovered online dating, it was if the clouds had opened. Was it possible? Was it possible I could wrap up all my training in poetry and writing, all the linguistic marketing wizardry I had honed for companies like Ogilvy and BMW, all the screenwriting skills I had cultivated as an Emmy-nominated producer and writer of several movies and TV shows—and attract women online with writing?

I not only could but I did, excavating site after site, meeting hundreds of fascinating women in my post-divorce frenzy. I had an ego to rebuild, after all, and in the process, came to a deeper and deeper understanding of what attracted men to women and women to men. As the frenzy settled and my intrigue grew, I wrote, almost as an afterthought, two detailed guidebooks[1] on how to attract what I call not the opposite sex, but the "complementary sex" online, and suddenly found myself with a global readership.

The core of what I had been teaching was that if you wrote a profile that spoke in a language the other gender could actually FEEL, then you could stand out from the crowd. Merit in writing was the key—how to communicate your humor, your heart, your gifts—in language that dazzled the eyes and stirred the hearts (and subtly, the loins) of your target market.

So when I got a call in 2012 from my friend, book agent Alicia Dunams, telling me about a new site called WhatsYourPrice.com, where generous men actually paid women to give them a shot by going on a first date with them, I scoffed. This was against all my principles. Everything I taught was how to develop yourself, deepen your emotional and adventurous life, and cultivate your ability to articulate yourself so the other

---

[1] Check out www.DeepOnlineAttraction.com for men and www.TheRightManOnline.com for women.

gender would feel the deep, beautiful, complex man or woman you are.

You weren't supposed to "buy" that attention. You were supposed to earn it.

But when Brandon Wade, CEO and founder of WhatsYourPrice.com, got on the phone with me, his earnestness in "defending the nerdy and skill-less" touched me. Brandon's story, which you will hear about in these pages, touched me. And as I began interviewing people who used the site, I came to see that there was a whole world of people there who valued exactly what WhatsYourPrice.com offered and could find it nowhere else. They were deeply grateful for it. It was a unique meeting forum, where money opened doors and created a kind of honesty and trust that other sites didn't.

There are many paths to the mountaintop of human intimacy, with all its various and complex faces. These are the stories of a group of hopeful lovers who took a novel path on their search for a relationship. And it is the story of their unlikely hero, a skinny, invisible uber-nerd who washed up on American shores from Singapore, burning not only with brilliance and ambition, but with the dream of one day, maybe, if he did things right...he could get a date.

Adam Gilad

Topanga, California
May 15, 2012

INTRODUCTION

"Wait—you mean I get PAID for going on a date?"

~

*"Come on, who are you fooling? Isn't that
straight-up prostitution?"*

~

*"Well, I'm the invisible man on
other sites. I'll give it a try."*

If ever there were an online dating site built to bring scorn raining down from all sides, WhatsYourPrice.com is it.

From men who are adept at dating, attractive, and social, you get, "What kind of loser would have to pay for a date!?"

From less-attractive women: "Sounds like high school all over again. The dumb cheerleaders get the guys everyone wants—only now it's guys with money, not muscles."

From men with empty pockets: "That sucks. Rich guys buy the hot girls and price me out of the market."

And from all corners: "Um...men are buying dates? There's a name for that—prostitution."

In the public mind, online dating has only recently climbed out of the muck. Just a few years ago, it was considered a desperate ploy by people who "couldn't get a date." That it was something other people "had" to do.

During its infancy, online dating seemed to be a scrim behind which suspicious men lurked and wanton women lured. Horror stories abounded, some of them even true. Everything seemed hidden, strange, dangerous, and probably perverted.

Then Web 2.0 came, and along with digital ubiquity, online dating became just another fueling station in our daily circling on the racetrack of electronic life. Our banking moved online. Our shopping. Google stomped into the landscape, revealing the tiniest details of our hidden world in its tyrannosaurus path. Facebook injected itself into our veins. The curtain between the private and the public realms was blown to dust, like the face of the villain in *Raiders of the Lost Ark.* The world changed, and suddenly, online dating was the norm.

In fact, nearly 20% of marriages are said to have found their conception in the "pixelated" barn dances and penny socials that are online dating sites.

Almost faster than we could understand its implications, online dating became the world's longest singles bar.

Except at *this* bar, with a thousand niches rising, with search engine optimization, public relations, media buying, and adwords aplenty, we have an army of carnival barkers shouldering hopeful singles through the doors with the subtlety of gloved Tokyo subway-stuffers.

In a world of cheap abundance, online dating has become the infinite well. If your date doesn't work out, if your girlfriend scorns you, if your boyfriend doesn't listen or if you're just alone one night at home and you get that ancient itch to connect your heart or your genitals to another set of same out there—this twenty-four-hour singles bar's doors are wide open. And folks, it's packed inside. You don't even need to flash your license to get in. You just need to flash your teeth in a photo or two and condense your gifts and your desires to a few choice words.

Everybody's welcome.

But not everybody succeeds.

I've been an inveterate online dater for ten years and an author of two books on how to do online dating right. I have seen how men and women sabotage themselves. I have coached men and women into bold self-expression leading to a newfound popularity and often, marriage. And I have seen thousands of people make a feint at online dating and retreat, feeling battered or ignored, and claiming that online dating "doesn't work".

Clearly, the numbers show, online dating *does* work. But it favors the attractive. It favors the hot bod. It favors the twenty-eight foot boat underfoot, the hip duds, the cool look. It favors the broad-chested and the full shock of hair.

But what happens online to the geeky guy with the heart of gold? He of the slight shoulders, the thick glasses—but the successful medical practice? What happens to the overworked, maybe slightly overweight guy who can't get a single woman to write back to him, who has no time to "work" Match.com or go out at night to meet women, but whose care and leadership makes him a hero to his thirty employees? What happens to the accomplished man in his late forties who has worked like a madman, built a nest, a fortune, and possesses a world of experience and wisdom—and now wants to start a family with an attractive young woman?

They discover that on the great online singles bar, they are relegated to the shadows at the back of the room just as they are offline, sipping their drinks, gazing enviously and forlornly at the Grade-A meat market—shimmering smiles, glimmering, moussed, highlighted hair, poppy biceps and square jaws—all jostling confidently under the spotlight.

How does a man, or woman, for that matter, who has worked hard, who is smart, who has created some success in the world, who knows his or her inner worth, but who is not blessed with Hollywood looks or what has become known as "approach mastery", get a place at the front of the line?

How does someone who is successful in every way—except the ways that commonly get first dates—get noticed by an attractive partner?

How can you, if you have everything to offer, except perhaps the face or the great opening line or the social fluency to stop a potential attractive mate and dazzle his or her attention in the first few seconds, get a shot?

There are two ways...

You can put in the time and the study to develop expertise at the art of the attraction—a rising soft science that dissects the dynamics of that initial encounter. As I teach it throughout my coaching books and programs, you can learn to articulate yourself boldly, wittily, with the penetrating ray of authentic humanity that is so rarely offered (more on that in Part III of this book). That'll often get you a shot.

Or you can shortcut the process and simply buy your shot.

That was the eureka moment that gave birth to What's Your Price.

In this book, you are going to see what led to this revelation in the mind of a brilliant MIT grad—himself a self-professed geek who couldn't get a date for the life of him—and how the very idea of What's Your Price has horrified some people and given new hope to a whole host of others.

What's Your Price scares people.

It scares people because it commodifies a cherished moment in our romantic narrative—that one area of our lives we fantasize to be free from monetary considerations.

On some level, we all want love to be pure. A magical, sacred meeting of soulmates who just "know" at that first moment that the angels are shepherding us into a lifetime of bliss.

Even though a 50% divorce rate should make us know better...

Even though the entire dance of attraction, dating, and romance has always been woven through with the green threads of lucre, and for very good and important reasons, which we will explore in the following pages...

Even though the idea of "buying" a date with an attractive dinner partner, for fifty bucks or two hundred, gives a whole cadre of love-seekers a novel opportunity to make their case in an extended conversation rather than relying on a Photoshopped profile picture or a "So, you come here often?" moment at a wine bar...

Even with all these things...

What's Your Price provokes extreme negativity in people.

After all, love should be blind, right? We should see each other for our true, unique, lovable selves, regardless of looks or investments, right? (But honestly, would you marry the Elephant Man, without a penny to his name, if he popped the question?) Money should never dirty the pristine bloom of love, right?

Yeah. Right.

And every mother is a saint. Every father an icon of propriety. Every business a shining example of noble individualism made good. And every politician, a true patriot who cares for the salt-of-the-earth citizen.

Despite the siren song of our better angels, we live in a world where money matters.

How we make money matter, however, is the essential question.

What's Your Price is an experiment. It uses money to open otherwise closed doors.

Is it susceptible to the greed and lust that flesh is heir to? Of course, sometimes.

Do some men think spending money over an evening entitles them to sex? Yes. Although the site explicitly warns them not to expect that.

Do some gold-digger women use to site to try to separate rich guys from their dollars for meals and vacations? You betcha.

Do some men lie about their age to try to score a hot young thing? About their height? Their wealth? Their girth? Of course they do.

These things happen *just as they do on all other sites*, and for that matter, in the *meatworld* (my favorite term for the non-online world, what we call "real life") as well.

Do some women accept dates with men they have no intention falling in love with, because they want a free dinner? Sure. Just as they do on other sites—and here, they'll happily take the 40 or 150 bucks in cash, too, thank you very much.

What's Your Price is not perfect. It's a relatively new forum that addresses a specific need, a specific pain, and a group of people who finally want a place at the table.

And they are willing to buy it.

What follows in these pages, I think, will surprise you. Just as hearing the stories of people's experiences on the site surprised me.

You will hear their voices, their frustration and hope, their cynicism, their realism, and their optimism. These are voices of experience, of the actual world, as far from the syrupy, manufactured Hallmark-world voices of puppies and cherubs.

"Love is stronger than death," the Song of Solomon reminds us.

You just need to give it a chance to find root.

And if that means laying down a C-spot for a couple of hours over a nice dinner, who are you to spit your scorn?

What's Your Price is an experiment. It's a place where a guy with B-team looks but perhaps an A-team personality gets a shot at winning the heart of an A-list-looking gal, which remains a universally hot market. Let's take a peek into the lab and see what is brewing...

Part I:
The Nerd's Bouquet

I Covered My Face in Shame as She Couldn't Stop Laughing

In 2009, What's Your Price was born in the imagination of Brandon Wade. In many ways, though, you could say its genesis came on a steamy tropical afternoon on a tiny Pacific island as he nervously paced outside his high school...

"I don't think a seventeen year old has ever felt as much shame. I was smart, the number one physics student in all of Singapore. I was on the Student Council, I did public speaking. Everybody in my school knew me—and I was 100% invisible to girls.

That didn't matter so much. What mattered was that I was 100% invisible to one particular girl: she was slim, graceful, an athlete. I watched her every day from afar, memorizing her gestures, her facial expressions, her schedule, building up a fantasy of us being together.

There was one problem—I had never spoken a word to her and was terrified. Finally, I couldn't stand it any longer. I was going to explode. I had to do something. So I went to my dad and told him my dilemma, admitting that I was too shy to approach her.

He told me, in his typical scientific way, that the issue was not shyness, but rather, "You're afraid of making a fool of yourself." It was simple logic. "If you go up to her, and if you fail, then you become the fool you were afraid of."

But that didn't stop me. I made my decision. I planned the whole thing out. I went to the library and to the bookstore and got every book about overcoming shyness. I made a plan to skip chemistry class because I knew she would be in the cafeteria at that exact time, working by herself, as she did every day. (Remember, I knew her every move!)

The fateful day arrived. I came to campus early and paced around the building in my school uniform under the tall coconut palms, in those brief hours before the air grew heavy and humid. I paced and I practiced, repeating what the books on shyness told me I should say, over and over. I was going to own up to being shy and say these exact words, right out of the book:

I don't normally do this. I'm usually very shy, but I had to come up and talk to you.

Those words would work! After all, the books promised.

I went to my morning classes and practiced

repeating those words during each break. My goal was monumental but simple—to walk up, to say the words, and to get to know something about her that day.

Then the right class period came and my palms grew sweaty. I slipped outside and peered in through the cafeteria window. There she was, right on schedule, in her beige school uniform, leaning over her books. Alone.

Ten minutes passed. Then twenty. Time seemed to race. I paced outside the windows, perfecting those few words, working up the courage, but felt no courage at all. Finally, I checked my watch and saw there were only five minutes left!

I didn't choose to go to her. My legs did. They carried me even though the rest of me was terrified. I got closer and closer and as I approached within a few feet, she looked up and...

I tripped, right in front of her. Flat on the ground. I could hear her laughing. I stared at the floor tile. I had to do this! The golden words cycled through my head. I reached up and yanked myself up to face her—and of course I stepped on her foot.

"Ow!" she yelled through her laughter.

"I am shy!" I shouted in her face, incongruously.

Now she was laughing even harder. Her beautiful eyes watered with scorn. Her perfect lips were helpless with ridicule.

I had done it. Exactly what my father said. I had proved that I was a fool, after all.

I covered my red face with my hands and stood there. After maybe a minute, I said a few things. I don't remember what. Then I hurried away.

After that, every time I saw her, I would walk the other way. I was a confirmed fool, as proven by my dad's theory. I was a fool, so I never talked to her again."

Should Your Awkward Eyeglasses Condemn You to a Life of Misery?

*"It's better to be looked over
—than it is to be overlooked."*
—Mae West

Intimacy is like oxygen.

If you have ever been held under water, you know your mind focuses. All you can think about is air. And so it is for so many people, arguably more so for men, that when we are deprived of intimacy, and more specifically physical intimacy. The hunger for it expands to fill the mind, the body, the will. It becomes an obsession.

Innumerable bad movies have been made about teens clambering over obstacles and each other to achieve their "first time". They are usually comedies, but in real life, the pain of unloved characters watching others find, cultivate, and enjoy intimacy—both sexual and emotional, while sitting on the sidelines of human connection—is no laughing matter.

Women generally find intimacy when they want it. They cuddle with each other better. They are more emotionally available to each other. And if they want even the simplest sexual stimulation, well, undo a couple of buttons, blow out your hair, and there are offers to be had at every corner bar and bistro. As Chris Rock hilariously explained it, every attractive woman since she's thirteen years old is consistently "being offered dick".

"Hey, can I get that door for you—want some dick!?"

For men, of course, it's not that easy. For a dozen reasons, women across most cultures are protective of their favors. And in this time of confusing gender roles, with women asserting themselves in a variety of ways, young men are confused about how assertive they should be with women. What's considered a masculine show of affection and what's sexual assault? What is appropriate? What is offensive? What's the line between confidence and arrogance? What's the line between vulnerable and non-masculine? Do women want the straight truth or do they want the dance of romance, with all its swoops and mis-directions? What do women want? Whom do they want to date? And why do they seem to make such bad choices (meaning *guys who are not me*)?

For generations, men's sexual imprinting has occurred during adolescence, when girls bloom into exotic, enticing, curvaceous bodily buffets. And to most young men, it seems that the obnoxiously bold, the athletic and the "bad boys" are the ones helping themselves and filling their plates, shouldering out the timid, reserved, gawky, and socially inept.

We tend to laugh compassionately at the image of a circle of teenage boys, huddled over a 1973 Playboy, trying to figure out what is what and what goes where. But do we allow ourselves to feel the pain of grown men who sit at home, depleting their credit cards to talk to webcam girls for a facsimile of female contact? Spending hours in anonymous chat rooms? High-diving into an omniverse of pornography where people seem to be copulating nonstop, in every position, location, and combination imaginable?

Female attention remains rare oxygen for millions of men who simply are not "good" at attracting women right off the bat, who have, what nerds might call, bad GUI (graphic user interface). These men don't have the social suavity, the hip garb, the easy conversation—and they lose out.

In her startlingly honest and, frankly, sad book, *Marry Him: The Case For Settling for Mr. Good Enough*, Laurie Gottlieb tells the tale of a generation of hip, smart, pretty women who dismissed man after man for wearing the wrong shirt, saying the wrong thing, using the wrong fork...and then waking up at age forty to discover that "all the good men were taken."

As she confesses, her own husband-shopping soon bloated into an ever-expanding list of demands:

"...the thinking would go: the last guy wasn't X, so the next time I want X, plus all the things I had on my list before. Basically, my Husband Store went from a six-story building to the world's tallest skyscraper. And I didn't think I was alone."

She was right! Among women she interviewed who found themselves unwantedly single at forty, she heard tales of the men they had passed up for all the wrong reasons, realizing later *that these same men had all the good qualities of a good husband.* However, at first blush they were...

      ✓ Too short
      ✓ Too wide
      ✓ What's up with those glasses?
      ✓ Not romantic enough
      ✓ He brought me flowers, but cheesy ones that spoke to bad taste
      ✓ Not exciting enough
      ✓ He had nose hairs
      ✓ Ear hairs
      ✓ Unkempt eyebrows
      ✓ Too weak
      ✓ Too predictable
      ✓ His voice was too low
      ✓ His voice was embarrassing—it was too high
      ✓ He was too cheery and optimistic
      ✓ He was losing his hair
      ✓ He used strange words like 'fabulosa'
      ✓ He loved me too much
      ✓ He had never seen *Casablanca*

Now it turns out these same women say they would settle for a guy with ANY hair—and yes, cheery and optimistic would be nice. In a hyper-competitive world where "deserve" became the new "desire," the most trivial things end up becoming decisive deal-breakers.

And so this generation of highly desirable and insanely demanding women turned up their noses at these un-tweezed, un-ideally-voiced *"men who had all the good qualities of a good husband."* And it turned out that many of those same men—socially awkward, physically non-alpha, wifeless, loveless, even sexless—quietly steered their energies where they were valued. Into building their careers and their companies.

While great, attractive, smart women keep their antennae high in the air for the surface signals of an attractive catch, they neglect the sonar of their deeper selves. And so, they miss out on all those great qualities that so many passed-over men possess, but cannot easily display in a quick bar introduction or next to a less-than-stellar online dating photo.

In some ways, as twenties blend into thirties and thirties accelerate into forties, the power balance begins to turn. Gottlieb tracks how reality has caught up to these women:

> *What would be their deal-breakers now? Someone with an addiction, someone who had a bad temper, someone who's unkind, someone who doesn't have a job, someone who's not warm or*

doesn't have a generous spirit, someone who's inflexible, someone who's irresponsible, someone who's dishonest, someone who wouldn't be a great father, someone who's old enough to be their own father. The rest, these women feel, is negotiable, but it's a realization that might have come too late…"

Slowly, it dawns on women that the geeky guy who loves his family and works hard might be a far better life partner than the boozy, chummy, former high-school football star salesman. Slowly, depth matters. But in our culture, depth does still face an uphill battle to get noticed.

Our culture is a funhouse gallery of shifting mirrors and shiny surfaces. We valorize the showy muscles of the arms over the steady muscle of the heart. We pay more attention to the highlights of hair than to the light that might be burning in another person's soul. We want to believe in instant magic. We celebrate the idea of "love at first sight" (e.g., love on the surface) over the arduous process of vetting another person's depth of character.

And so, Brandon, brilliant as he was in the sciences, found himself awkward, isolated, and virtually invisible in his new country of America. Let's flash forward seven years from that horrible day in Singapore…

"So here I was, a recent MIT graduate—two degrees including an MBA. I was making good money. I had an adventurous spirit but I was among men all day and didn't know how to meet girls. I'm skinny, I'm Asian—before it started being cool to be an Asian man. I was a total nerd with big, oversized glasses and I was lonely. It was 1994. A friend of mine paid $8,000 for a matchmaker but got nowhere. I, too, joined a matchmaking agency—remember, this was before the web. They had a huge video library. I went into their office and had to record a video of myself. Then I had to sit there to view videos of single women and write down which ones I'd like to meet. I had to sign a one-year contract. It cost $200 to $300 bucks a month. I didn't get a single date."

When online dating came around, his luck didn't improve. "I wrote a million women—no response." What's worse, his work in the tech field didn't make meeting women during the normal workday that easy...

"Back in the day, before computers, Internet or Smartphones, there was just a lot more social interaction. You had no choice. But that's changed. It's become too easy to hide behind a computer or an iPhone. I started chatting online

with women, but that's not the same thing as dating. That's still a whole different skill set. And I never even had the chance to develop it. I couldn't get a date."

From Motorized Ducks To A Monster Insight

"When we cherish something, we pay for it."

Wade worked for a while as a consultant with the reputable firm Booz Allen. (He spent a few years as one of the youngest executives at General Electric, where Bob Nardelli, the same man who later became CEO of Home Depot and Chrysler, was his mentor. He had even sat across from GE's legendary CEO Jack Welch and publicly disagreed with him.) But while these experiences sharpened his business skills, this kind of job wasn't satisfying. He had developed a fierce entrepreneurial spirit. He wanted more creativity, more control. He didn't like the idea that he could be laid off at the whim of someone else.

So in the late 90s, he waded into the booming dot-com economy. With a group of friends, his enterprising forays swelled and shrank with astonishing rapidity, and in, in good faith, he actually returned cash to investors when he realized the dot-com crash was going to wipe them all out.

For a short while, as he tells it, he "took refuge" at Microsoft, but that didn't last.

He wanted to create his own company and soon founded a novelty tourist company with his best friend.

This was Bay Quackers—the San Francisco Duck Tours, which offered curious visitors to the foggy city an amphibious vehicle with which to take it all in. Full of the zest of creating businesses, he soon thereafter formed a second company that would change his life— and oddly, become the genesis of What's Your Price.

San Francisco was at that time, and still is, awash in engineers, flooded in tech types and all the supporting cast tech startups attracted. Most of them were tossed out of their overpriced office suites with the fall of the NASDAQ. Cannily, Wade started an employment service.

But he added a clever reversal of the standard service, as exemplified by the biggest player in the field, Monster.com. Instead of having an employer pay to post an ad, Wade thought, why not make it free for employers to post, and have the throngs of job-seekers pay for access to the job offers?

Through his friends and contacts, Wade ascertained that every decent job offer drew dozens or hundreds or even *thousands* of applicants. It cost nothing for every hapless aspirant to e-mail a resume, and so HR departments found themselves buried in messages from hopeful employees.

Wade calculated that the balance of supply and demand seemed to favor charging the applicants rather than the job offers. It was the job seekers who were more desperate. Would they pay to get a competitive advantage? "When you pay fifty bucks to apply," Wade reasoned, "it narrows your market." In other words, those who toss their feather to the wind and hope to turn up with fortune on their side stop tossing feathers when it costs them fifty dollars a toss. The serious applicants, the ones who are truly right for the job, pony up. Their resumes thus get a greater chance to be seen, and employers don't have to wade through mountains of spurious applications. The right people get a fair hearing for the right job—and efficiency gets served.

Things started to go well for Wade. But despite his financial advances and business acuity, his love life was not finding comparable success. "I had zero luck on traditional dating sites like Match.com or Yahoo! Personals, and not much more on Millionaire Match, either. Free sites such as Plenty of Fish bore even worse results." Problem-solver that he is, Wade figured he could create his own site. After all, what better way to meet women?

One fact is well known. On most dating websites, men greatly outnumber women. As Wade watched his own sister receive over 600 messages during her first two days on Yahoo! Personals, his intrigue only grew. He asked her how she chose whom to respond to, and she told him, "Well, I just scan through the men quickly. If they have an attractive picture I read the profile and message. If he has a decent job and if he writes an interesting response to mine, I would continue."

Out of the 600 messages she received, how many did she respond to? Less than fifteen. That is a 2.5% response rate, which while better than Brandon was getting, still seemed miserably low. There must, he considered, be a lot of men out there who were similarly frustrated.

To solve his—and now, clearly, others'—dating problems, he decided, he must first find a solution to this persistent imbalance. There were just so many more men than women on each site. How could a guy without muscles and a great jawline break through all the white noise?

The big ah-ha moment, fascinatingly, came not from studying the dance of dating; it came from mulling the imbalances of the employment market, thinking about the willing-to-pay horde of hungry job seekers chasing a few attractive jobs. He hit upon the idea of applying what he'd learned to his own, personal, dating challenge. There had to be men like him who had financial resources but who were no good at approaching or attracting women up front. And these men were probably equally hungry to meet them. And would probably pay to do so.

And suddenly, Brandon Wade, nerd extraordinaire, diligent and enterprising young tech entrepreneur, found himself in a new world. A new world that, is, in fact, one of the oldest and most universal worlds, though it remains a discreet one. The world of Sugar Daddies and Sugar Babies...

Around 2006, I took that (employment) software engine and turned it into [the site] SeekingArrangement.com, to solve my own problem. I was trying to figure out how to take the idea of "generous" men that I learned from my mother and create a business around it. I punched in the terms "wealthy generous man," which, to me, was a term of respect and responsibility, and 'sugar daddy' came up. I didn't know about the world of sugar daddies—I only discovered it when I searched for keywords for my new dating site idea. I didn't even know the words—'sugar daddy' and 'sugar baby.'

SeekingArrangement.com was something new for Wade, although the idea of generosity with which he began the company was not. In fact, it was very traditional for him, dating back to his childhood.

I didn't grow up with the same idea of material equality that we have here in the States. My dad was from a poor family; my mother was from a wealthy family. But that didn't matter. My dad worked very, very hard and raised himself up. My mom, though educated, stayed home to be a housewife and raise me and my sister. And he gave her a household monthly allowance, which is traditional in Singapore. It's the accepted way of a man providing for his family.

Now, my mother loved beautiful things, as women so often do. Sometimes, she would take me out—and with her own family money—she would show me jewelry that she wanted and bought it for herself. "You MUST be generous to your wife, one day, Brandon," she would tell me. "A good man is generous!"

One day, and I will never forget this, when I was only seven years old, she took me out shopping with her as she always did, but this time she was very agitated. She stopped me on the street and took me by my small shoulders and told me in a very harsh way, "Never once since we were married did I get any jewelry from your dad. He is responsible, but make sure you never treat your woman this way! Be generous! Take care of her! Buy her beautiful things!'

That day she bought herself a particularly nice piece of jewelry. My father noticed it and got angry. "Who bought you this!?" he yelled.

"I did," she said, crying. Her sadness was mixed with anger. "Since you won't, I bought it myself!"

I absorbed all my mom's pain in that moment. It was clear to me that it wasn't about the jewelry. It was about not feeling valued by my father. So I learned early that gifts and generosity are one of the main and most traditional languages of love.

Of course, now I understand so much more—if you've read the book The Five Love Languages *by Dr. Gary Chapman, which I recently read along with my wife, you know that along with gifts, kind words of appreciation, actions of service, quality time, and touch are each important love languages.*

For Wade, at this point, ill-versed in the finer arts of love's expression, material generosity was the primary and perfectly natural expression of a man's affection.

When he founded SeekingArrangement.com,

I was no millionaire. I never had been. But I always helped the girls I liked with their homework, with resumes. I'd chip in for rent if they needed. This kind of relationship where you do nice things for each other—including gifts of money when needed—was not new to me. Seeking Arrangement wasn't that unlike my life and the lives of my tech friends or even unlike my parents. My mother still gets a monthly allowance from my father all these years later, even though she has her own money.

The first decade of the 21st century may have been a bust in several other fields, but it was boom time for online dating. Mobility, isolating jobs, and the general ubiquity of online transactions proved to be fertile soil for companies like Match.com, JDate, Plenty of Fish—and SeekingArrangement.

Within the first two weeks, the site SeekingArrangement.com grew to two thousand members and it was only then that Brandon started charging membership fees.

By the end of the first year, they reached 150,000 users with a ratio of ten women to every man. By 2012, Seeking Arrangement had become the world's largest sugar daddy dating website, with over 1.3 million members worldwide.

Seeking Arrangement was founded on two very simple premises. First, that there are lots of men with lots of money and little skill, time, patience, or desire to cultivate a profound love relationship, who would happily pay a woman to win her instant attention. Some men are perfectly willing to take women to expensive restaurants, to take them on trips and to romance them something like the way the Beast wooed the Beauty, with gifts and traditional chivalry—and perhaps revealing his true heart. And some men and women prefer the stipend model, similar to that which you find in the old world, more or less, where she receives a regular payment for her time and attention.

The second premise is that there are plenty of women who for reasons of education, opportunity, chance, simple choice, financial devastation, or bad choices—want to date richer men. To be frank, there are plenty of women who are motivated simply by opportunism, fun, adventure or thrill-seeking, who also want or need to lift themselves out of their current situation by dating richer men.

At first blush, it's easy to dismiss sites like Seeking Arrangement as thoroughly crass. As a kind of stealthy e-whoredom. And yes, putting women on retainer for their affections falls well outside our conventional and accepted notions of how sex and love should, ideally, be connected. No one would mistake it for SeekingSoulmate.com.

But the truth is, when you start talking to people in "arrangements", a whole panoply of needs, desires, and complex human stories emerge. For example, though hard times may lead them into accepting money for a sexual relationship, many women do not see that big a difference between a long term "arrangement" and marriage. Perhaps it's not the "ideal" marriage of two souls, but the arid landscape of marriage that seems to make this ideal rare anyway.

Also, though sexual frustration, busy schedules, and dry marriages may drive men into paying for affection, companionship, and sex over a period of time in order to experience a facsimile of a relationship, it turns out

that people—men and women—will in fact drift more
deeply into love, even though the relationship may
begin with an agreement over little but cash. It turns
out that people often fall in love in arranged marriages
in countries like India. So too, what starts as an
"arrangement" on a site like Seeking Arrangement may
too develop into a enduring heart allurement.

Seeking Arrangement is a busy and prosperous site.
For members, bills and tuitions get paid. Egos get
stroked. Paid vacations are taken. Adventures had.
Long-term companionships blossom. Lonely hearts are
soothed. Bodies find each other. Marriages happen. Men
pay for attention, aspire for sexual attention, but as all
parties are free to choose what they choose, nothing is
guaranteed. As has been often lamented, how is *that* so
different from some marriages?

The bottom line is that among the broad spectrum of
consenting adults, there seem to be a wide range of
"arrangements" that work. Enough, certainly, to make
sugar daddy sites like Seeking Arrangement multi-
million dollar marketplaces for the practical-minded,
the lonely, the adventurous, the open-minded, as well as
the greedy and the needy.

With Seeking Arrangement, Wade had succeeded in
bringing together generous men with women who
otherwise had little or no access to wealth. The dawn of
the electronically facilitated sugar daddy culture was
on. But it wasn't long that he began to hear more and

more from his customers about a trend, one that caught his attention.

Wade is an unusual CEO, often blogging and talking to his customers. "People—both men and women—complained on Seeking Arrangement that they wanted actual relationships, serious relationships, not just pay-for-play 'arrangements'." Sites like Match had an increasing lock-hold on standard dating. Could there be something in between? How might he bring together generous men and attractive women without them having to enter the world of sugar daddies and mere "arrangements".

Wade, the consummate dating outsider, was finding himself wandering closer into the realm of a very traditional kind of matchmaking, where for men, the currency is money, and for women, the significant currency is physical beauty.

According to Wade, in considering this question, he reflected back on his own pain, his MIT days and all those years after when he was still cripplingly shy. And again, as typical of him, he came up with a technology solution to a personal problem.

Something was clearly wrong with the matching system on sites like Match.com; again, I noticed it was the same problem with job sites. Thousands of applicants applying for a few select, attractive jobs—and never hearing back. So I thought, what if

I can beef up the supply side of the equation by making the site free for the women—and now, even add a financial incentive for women to join? Wouldn't I get a higher quality of woman, or at least a higher number of them?

And then, what if, as I did in the employment world, I made the "seekers" pay rather than the "attractive" component, "generous" in the jobs world being the job seekers and "attractive" being job opportunities that are in high demand. Here, the "seekers" would be the generous men. After all, they are the hungry ones. They are the ones who are personally incentivized to get some success where they couldn't succeed on other sites. What if a little bit of offered money leveled the playing field? What if they could "buy" a place at the dating table?

At first, it was just an idea. No one had tried anything like this before. Not being a guesser, but rather a scientist by nature, a numbers guy, Wade quickly hired a market research firm and brought a cross-section of women into a hotel room in Las Vegas, near his offices. The women ranged in age from 18 to 55 and represented a broad spectrum of economic and educational strata.

Wade and the research firm conducted the experiment methodically, not knowing what to expect.

He recounts the story with palpable relish…

One by one, we showed the women various photos of men—not Brad Pitt quality—and asked them, "Would you date this guy? How about this guy? Would you give this guy a shot? Would you accept a first date with him if he asked?"

If they said "no," we asked them "why not?" Sometimes they said, they don't have enough time to date men that didn't attract them right off the bat. So we'd ask, "But how do you know you don't like him until you meet him?"

The women would shrug. They really didn't have a good answer for that. Women, I think, more instinctively know that it takes time to discover if someone is a good match or not, but they, like everybody else, were taking the easy way out. They wanted it all, and on first glance.

Then it got really interesting. We'd ask, "Okay, so this guy you said no to—what if we offered you forty bucks to give him a shot? No? How about sixty dollars? How about $100 to have dinner with him? What about $150?

And what we learned was for almost every woman, at some point, the money was too good to refuse. There is a magic number where looks and profile and compensation combine, where it makes sense to them to say, "Sure. I've got nothing to lose.

Maybe he'll be good company. All right. I'll go on a date with him."

Wade learned other things in the market research room, most notably how many women had high anxiety about their cost of dating. He had never considered this before. He discovered that one of the reasons women often refused to accept a date with a man they didn't consider highly attractive at first sight was a monetary one. Going on dates not only costs men money, it costs women also. Women told him that it could cost up to $70 to go on a date. They reeled off the costs—from laundry and dry cleaning to hair and make-up, to baby-sitters and taxis and in some cases, lost hours at home-based jobs.

In addition, women experienced increased stress on first dates over whether a man was going to pay the bill or insist on splitting the bill. Dating was not the free ride for women that it's often portrayed to be, so they had to pick and choose carefully who they would go out with. And so they were less willing to give a fairly or less-attractive guy a chance. He'd have to have what they call in the computer world "good GUI", or graphical user interface. In other words—if he was a hottie to them, he had a better chance of landing that first date.

Wade added those concerns into his calculations. In any business transaction, he figured, if the perceived return outweighs the costs, it becomes natural to say yes and move forward. So if you can take away a woman's anxiety by diminishing her risk and upping the ante of guaranteed reward, you'd get more attractive women accepting more dates with hopeful, generous men. For Wade, it was sound business practice translated into the world of dating.

He took the data from this survey and excitedly gathered his employees at Seeking Arrangement and laid out what he had discovered. His hunch seemed to make sense. He wanted his staff to pull apart the idea if they could, but they didn't. Looking over the results, they all seemed to agree that it could work.

And so WhatsYourPrice.com was born—as was a new calculus of attraction.

In the everyday world, different men have different advantages. A smooth lothario might show up on a girl's doorstep with a flourish of red roses and a hand-scripted poem. An athlete might impress her by swinging her high and dropping her gingerly into the front seat of his convertible. A minstrel Romeo might sing serenades under her bedroom window, or, more likely these days, from the stage of a local open-mic.

But what of the nerd? What's he supposed to do? Solve a Rubik's Cube in under a minute before her bedazzled eyes? Explain the energy potential of algae as she swoons? Show her the schematics of his microchip innovations?

Sure. He could try.

But now, with What's Your Price, he could arrive with something of substance, the universal equalizer—not a spray of flowers, but cold, hard cash.

Call it the Nerd's Bouquet.

Now he would just have to see if it would work...

Part II:
WYP: Launch, Perception, and Reality

"Whoever said money can't buy happiness
didn't know where to shop."

—Robin Kramer, owner of
New York clothing boutiques

The Mechanics of WYP: How it Works

There are two categories of daters on WhatsYourPrice.com: the "generous" and the "attractive". Both of those terms can be self-defined. Generous might be $50 for one man or $400 for another. Everything is relative. There is no universal standard. And as for what is "attractive", Wade points out:

> *A slippery issue is the "attractive" designation. We at WYP do not define who is or is not attractive, nor do members have to go through any kind of "test"—as if such a thing existed! The category is purely subjective; almost anyone might feel comfortable calling themselves attractive. On the other hand, we've all known devastatingly beautiful people who actually consider themselves bad-looking! Beauty, as they say, is in the eye of the beholder.*

The process begins when a generous man[2] logs on

---

[2] In theory, a generous woman could seek out an attractive man, but, for the time being, the balance is skewed the other way. Also, gay daters comprise about 7% of the membership and contact each other. To represent the majority of members in the proportion to which they apply, and mostly because any other way would make for contorted and confusing sentences, for the remainder of this book, we are going to use "generous" and "man" interchangeably, and "attractive" and "woman" to mean the same thing. This is convenience of writing, not a judgment nor a negation of generous women/attractive men or of gay members.

and buys a certain amount of credits. He then gets access to peruse the profiles of attractive women and when he finds someone he would like to date, he offers her an amount (usually between $40–$150, depending on a variety of factors we will explain below).

The woman then has three choices. She can refuse his offer altogether and the story ends there. She can counter his offer, raising the amount. Or she can accept his offer.

Alternatively, the attractive woman can review all the generous men on the site and if she finds someone she might like to date, she can wink at him—inviting an offer—or suggest a number herself. Just as women have three choices when a man makes an offer, he can lower her offer, refuse, or accept it.

Once an amount is agreed upon, two things happen. If he chooses to communicate with her, his account is debited a certain number of credits based on the amount of the offer. And secondly, a conversation box is unlocked and the two can begin e-mailing each other, exchanging phone numbers, and arranging a date just as on any other web site.

It is important to understand that there are several filters between the man and the woman right at the start. The parties cannot communicate or meet until both parties have taken proactive steps to facilitate it. There is the matter of agreeing on the amount of the price for the date. There is the ability for a woman to refuse the offer and there is the small expenditure for the man to "unlock" a conversation.

Finally, if they begin to write and speak by phone, and one party decides he or she doesn't like the other, the deal is off. No one is obliged to go on a date. In fact, there is no obligation at all.

However, once they both show up for a date, then they have a contract, and the generous party is obliged to make the transaction—that is, to pay the attractive party the agreed-upon offer amount, in addition to footing the bill for the date.

It can sometimes get awkward here for the daters, since no other site creates this particular door-opener. Nobody expects the guy to toss greenbacks across the table, nor slide it across like some kind of smooth-handed croupier.

To ease the transaction, What's Your Price offers many ideas on how to transfer the "payment" for the date to the attractive partner, but usually a sweet greeting card with a short thank you note with cash tucked inside does the trick. It's fairly discreet, even if it feels kind of like your grandmother slipping you a ten-spot at Christmas. Nevertheless, it's the most popular way of getting this part over with. The generous man has a nifty opportunity here to add a heartfelt thought or two, and there is no green flashed in public, which might give other restaurant patrons the wrong idea.

Is this odd? Well, yes! This part is different from your average first date. In fact, to many on the outside, the exchange of actual money raises all kinds of red flags. But by the time you read the stories of the daters on WYP below and as we dig into the various "meanings" that money has for different people, I suspect you will agree that the exchange of cash for time on a first date opens more cultural questions than closes them.

Nevertheless, the temptation to judge the transaction as crass or tawdry is there. Prostitution is exchange of money for sex, which the WYP transaction is *definitively not.* There are plenty of places, online and off, where people can pursue that.

WYP is money for a first date. End stop. She can say no. He can say no. During the first date, the magic of chemistry may happen or not. And once the first date ends, if the couple wants to see each other again, there is no expectation of an exchange of cash for her time.

Money opens the door. It does not line every inch of the road into the future. Nor is there the expectation of a "happy ending" awaiting the generous man at the end of the night. In fact, in multiple places on the site read the words:

*Note: Sex should **never** be expected on the first date.*
Please be respectful to all members.

That's the fundamental intention and structure of the site.

Simple, no? Everyone should pretty much agree on what the site is for, no?

Well...no.

Not even close.

The Adam Smith of Dating

As expected, WYP launched to a flurry of curiosity, false assumptions, and outrage. But membership multiplied quickly and it was clear from the start that the site had instant appeal to certain personality types—beyond Brandon's ideal "nerd".

To begin, it had an appealing practical aspect for many women frustrated with other sites. Lauryn, a writer, editor, and adventurer, age 40, found the prospect of getting paid for a date both provocative and soothing...

> *I'd been on Match on and off a long time. I'm really looking for my guy and one day I saw a What's Your Price ad online. I was a little taken aback at first and I asked—is this even legal? Then I laughed. I thought, sure, I want to get paid if a first date totally sucks and if it's a good first date, all the better! Either way, I win.*

Other female members echo her matter-of-fact approach. Deborah is a 38-year-old divorced nurse...

> *Have you dated? I could shoot myself. At this point, I feel I deserve payment given the high probability that a first date could be a dud. If it's*

going to be a big, huge waste of time, at least I'm going to get paid for it. A lot of these guys are wealthy, and I think my time is as valuable as theirs.

Some were outright delighted at the whole concept...

It feels like, Wow! These guys want to pay money to go out with me? It's worth paying money just to be with me? I signed up right away.

Some were just curious. Alan is a 33-year-old political consultant...

I joined out of curiosity about what kind of women I'd find on the site. So far I've spent $200 for five first dates—two of the women returned the money. It's a relatively trivial amount, and it definitely makes it easier to get attractive women to go out with you. I think the money is probably a lot more important if the date goes badly.

And not surprisingly, it appealed to men who were busy and found that the popular dating sites were impenetrable and took far too much work. In fact, a significant proportion of male members are not "nerd" types at all. They are business owners who find the businesslike atmosphere that a money exchange creates to be a familiar and amenable habitat. They appreciate the time-saving "let's get down to the business of meeting" nature of the site. Doug, 35, works in tech near San Diego...

> *I joined Match.com and yes, I even joined OKCupid, but the level of women there was lower. Maybe I could have met someone on those sites but I didn't have the patience to get on there and work it day in and day out. There are a million guys all chasing the same twenty hot women. I run a business in two cities and I'm raising two daughters on my own. I've got no time to sift through BS profiles and write long-winded e-mails about how I like to walk on the beach. I want to know what a woman looks like, get an idea of her education, and her seriousness about finding a quality partner—and if that all adds up, I'm more than happy to lay down a hundred bucks to meet her for dinner. To me, it's a no-brainer. It's cheaper than the time and frustration other sites cost me.*

A quick perusal of testimonials on the dating site itself shows that this is one of the most valued advantages of the site...

> *I clicked on the pay your 20-credit fee button for*

the first time yesterday. And not even eleven minutes into today I can say I had my first date from WhatsYourPrice.com. This is a feat unmatched by ANY other dating website. Yes, I had to swallow my ego and pay to have a first date, but I actually got my first date, unlike my profiles on Match or PoF or TRUE or OKCupid or eHarmony or Yahoo Personals, which never get a reply...

***

I have been on so many other sites...but THIS ONE WORKS! However, it has created a bit of a time-management problem for me. Other sites, my response rate was low, maybe 10 percent, 15 at most. Here it is closer to 60 or 70 percent. So, I suddenly find myself totally overcommitted for dates with attractive, beautiful ladies... Oh well, there are worse problems to have, I suppose... I hope those ladies can be patient to wait...

***

So on Wednesday I started my profile. Before I finished it and 24 hours before my photos were approved I had two dates.

***

I have been a member for 4 days, and already have 3 dates lined up. I may have made too many offers! Who thought this would be so effective? I am very impressed. I will let you know how my dates go!

***

You guys should go on Howard Stern! This is the ONLY dating site that really works. It took me months to years to get a date on other sites, and it took me a day on here.

***

Within the first 10 days I have been on four dates through the site, and what's interesting is that the money aspect means something different each time. I had one date give me back my money...the next morning. In bed.

Men weren't the only ones driven by a taste for efficiency. While knee-jerk public perception sometimes suspects that women go on the site simply to "make" money, many women view the cash as little more than a shortcut to getting to the truth. Rebecca, 35, is a self-professed science nerd, an author with a strong spiritual bent, who is looking for a husband only...

On other sites, like Match.com—it was really random. You get so many people, unfiltered, all saying the same pre-fab little story lines. It's hard to distinguish anything from anyone, they're all saying the same thing and it tells you nothing about who they really are. It's got really poor odds, and just tons of random encounters.

I really appreciate traditional courtship. I am a .dy and enjoy being treated to open doors, a steady arm, and the confidence that a man of experience can provide.

On WYP, if he says, 'Hey I'm a generous man. I like to look after a woman and I like to impress upon her my competency, my capability, I'm self-made'—that eliminates a lot of other people who aren't that confident. WYP has better odds—the date happens fast, the truth comes out fast.

Tracy is a young college student...

I saw the ad 'Get paid to date' and that is my favorite thing about WYP. It gives me release, knowing that even if it's a horrible date, I'm gonna get paid for it. As a girl, you spend hours getting ready to please someone. I spent 3 hours for my first date, it was nice, we had a good time even though there wasn't a lot of chemistry. He had fun, I had fun. He paid me $200, which I guess wasn't much for him. And even though we didn't click, I didn't feel it was a waste.

Tracy, as it happens, is still dating the second man she met on the site, and is four months into a relationship. But whereas women like Rebecca took a shine to the practical advantages of What's Your Price, others—looking in from the outside—were not so forgiving.

Press, ratings, page impressions, and book sales are driven by controversy and from the start, there was no shortage of self-proclaimed experts and pundits ready to share their opinions through the media, without trying out the site. Not surprisingly, they've leaned heavily toward the negative, ranging from amusement to contempt to moral outrage.

Salon, the well-known online magazine, published a wink-wink style hack job by a writer named Tracy Clark-Flory. In it, she refers to the men on the site as "damaged goods" and "losers". Typical of the tone:

> *So it brings people together willing to pay and to be paid for a "date."*
>
> *Yes, yes, back in your day they had places like that too!*
>
> *They were called, brothels or "whorehouses" but damn it, this is the New Day and a New Age, and there's no offer of sex, just a date.*
>
> *So sweet, so innocent!"*

But a quick look at the comments thread below her article on the *Salon* site demonstrates the public's broader (and more forgiving) set of perspectives...

What were dowries if not economic exchanges?

To what end other than economics have the mothers of would-be brides calculated the worth and prospects of would-be grooms since time immemorial? Keeping a companion has always had a price tag, since the dawn of civilization, and it has always been possible to calculate that price to a fair degree of precision. Just because we're doing these things on the Internet now doesn't mean that they are different or novel.

—Amity

Bride prices. Dowries. Pre-nups. Marriage is a financial arrangement. Of course men pay more as they get older. I know of a wealthy guy who was dating two younger women. He was told that they were dating him for his money. His reaction was basically: And? That's why I have money, to get what I want. Really, when have men not used possessions and power as status symbols to reach the top of the reproductive totem pole and have access to the best women? Any five year old who watches Cinderella *or* Beauty and the Beast *can tell you exactly how this works. A girl's face is her fortune. Let's not pretend this is new or somehow shocking.*

—Anon

Why would a woman not choose a man who can make life easier for her? Women have the advantage of being able to date up the income ladder and, if I could, I would not hesitate to date up, either. However, women are somewhat disadvantaged in the workplace, so I don't think they have the better deal.

—Grapeable

Over on Fox TV, Bill O'Reilly, sitting with two news blondbots, did a short segment and raised ire by introducing the site as one that was "raising ire". Blondbot #1 immediately launched into an attack, calling WYP "sexist on its face...this is prostitution!" However, Blondbot #2 thought it sounded like "a fun twist on Match—men never get dates on other sites!"

At that point in the fast-paced exchange, the sexism-convinced blondbot revealed what I have seen to be a common, hostile "geekist" response to the site—particularly among beautiful people. Outraged, even palpably repulsed, she *exclaimed...*

...for $100 you're going to go out for three hours with a geek?

Is that really so horrible, oh coiffed one? Aren't geeks sexy in this age of Silicon Valley visionaries?

Hadn't Simon Pegg, the great British comic actor, gone on record confessing that…

Being a geek is all about being honest about what you enjoy and not being afraid to demonstrate that affection. It means never having to play it cool about how much you like something. It's basically a license to proudly emote on a somewhat childish level rather than behave like a supposed adult. Being a geek is extremely liberating.

Indeed, it turns out, to many women, finding refuge from a landscape of repressed, aggressive, socially-competitive and frustrated men, geeks can be extremely refreshing.

Wade is a firm believer in the good hearts of nerds and geeks everywhere. He gets emotional when people who are socially suave dismiss them. On the other hand, he doesn't seem bothered by the criticism of the site, although he often finds it unjust. What surprises him is the source of the attacks. He thought it would come from conservatives…

I'm always amazed how it's the more liberal people who are so outraged by the site. It's the conservatives, strangely enough, who seem to get it. When What's Your Price was discussed on The

O'Reilly Factor, the Republican woman thought it was a good idea! I thought the liberals would be more open-minded! I guess it makes sense—I'm letting the market do its work. That's why I've been called the Adam Smith of dating! I like that!

Perhaps it is not only the "free market" aspect of WYP that divides conservatives and liberals. One would suspect that there is a more idealistic notion of equality and fairness on the left, and that money shouldn't, in an ideal demo of equals, favor some over others. Another reason the left seems to be the source of most of WYP's criticism might be that many of those on the left tend not to gravitate to careers that are financially rewarding, such as social work, teaching, etc., the kinds that prioritize non-monetary rewards such as social service and the commons. That can create a natural jealousy of the rich. As one commentator under the O'Reilly YouTube clip forlornly put it…

Nice luck getting a date in the future when everyone is broke, guys. Every girl will have their price on a website. America has now declared itself as a harem to the few rich.

In January 2012, Wade appeared on the Anderson Cooper Show. Interestingly, the audience was very open to the concept of the site. They gave a palpable "Awww" when one of the show's guests—a WYP member—said he had a second date coming up with a woman he met, and again when a guy said his date gave him his money back at the end of their first date because she had such a good time.

But at the same time, some of the audience members were suspicious, raising familiar concerns about Internet dating safety. One asked a woman WYP member—a flight attendant well into her forties—if it was her "only source of employment". Reasonable questions were raised about the relationship between how much a man pays for a first date and what his expectations would then be.

But, as with the Fox blonde, that disturbing, strong note of contempt crept out at the idea that some people just don't have the social skills for easy dating. "Why don't you develop social skills?" one audience member demanded of a man using WYP who'd volunteered to appear on the show. Another woman castigated him. "Aren't you ashamed that the only thing that gets you a date is buying it?" Insisted another, "A high quality man is a man who is secure enough to use social skills to win over a woman, not his wallet."

In the best of all possible worlds, well, yes.

These audience members seemed to miss the point that the site was specifically built for men who, by definition, do not have the social skills to approach attractive women in common social settings. (It should be pointed out that Wade has made several inquiries to his subscribers about how he can provide dating coaching services to help members increase their social skill sets and is planning a suite of such services in the future.) The audience's hostility felt rather like a mansion-dweller spitting on a homeless man for not building an entertainment room in his split-level.

But the most negative force on the show was psychologist and "relationship expert" Dr. Michelle Callahan. She launched into a barrage of charges about the site that, significantly, began with her repeated, unsubstantiated phrase, "I don't believe…"

"I don't believe people are actually finding relationships on this site," she said. And, "I don't believe that it operates as a dating site, but rather as a euphemistic escort site."

Her beliefs notwithstanding, the escort charge is a common one. In response, Wade detailed that he and his staff screen profiles one by one as they come online and that he has a strict policy against solicitation of sex for money. He reminded Callahan that there are clear warnings about escorts being prohibited, as well as nudity in photos, and that if a member reports soliciting, "We take action. We kick them off." And in my interviews with men who have written Wade about women who solicited them on his site, these women, were, indeed, immediately removed.

That being said, there clearly are women on the site who are looking for sugar daddy relationships, with all that might entail. It could be for a night or it could be for an ongoing relationship. Of course, this occurs on all dating sites, from Craigslist all the way to the Millionaire dating sites and is impossible to prevent, as the language is often coded. And even though many of the initial members came from ads that Wade listed on his other sites (notably Seeking Arrangement, which leans toward a culture of mutual pampering), the WYP site is designed for something else entirely.

Dr. Callahan admitted that she understood escorting was not Brandon's original intention, but that it was there. As a psychologist, she offered, perhaps with some overstatement, her concern that people are coming to buy or sell sex and that could be "traumatic".

After the airing of the episode, the Anderson Cooper site comments section lit up. The men for whom Wade had built the site spoke up, hurt and offended by the tone of those on the show who castigated those who couldn't win over a woman with their social skills...

This is a ridiculous notion [from] the psychologist that was brought in to evaluate the criteria for...prostitution... She is a young, pretty, highly successful doctor. It's not hard to see she is getting dates... I'd like to believe that most people won't accept what she is saying....

Observed another...

I like how all the people who are against this site are all nice-looking and would have no problem getting a date.

Wrote one man who identified himself only as "Nerd":

I know women that will never give a nerd a chance. This site opens the door... I consider myself a nerd and I have the hardest time...getting a first date. I would not mind paying.

And from the autism spectrum came this comment:

I appreciate this website because it gives individuals who have Asperger's syndrome an opportunity for dating. As a woman with Asperger's, I would have definitely signed up for this because I don't have social skills, but I do have intellectual ability. A lot of 'nerds' out there [are people who] do have Asperger's; one of the diagnostic criteria...is social deficiency. We aspies/nerds desire love and relationships, but are often so impaired that it never happens. We cannot just be taught social skills. [A] site like this

would be very helpful in [helping us] find love."
—*Asperger's Syndrome*

For some who wrote in, lack of dating skills apparently can be as debilitating as brain disorders...

I am a 48-year-old male and have never once in my life been on an actual date. The rare times I've gotten the guts to ask someone out, I've been rejected. I would pay someone to go out on a date with me and I have no problem doing so. I am not a socially inept person, but I've just never had any skills when it comes to dating. I know there may be some underlying issue, but paying for a date doesn't seem like a bad idea to me at this stage of my life.

—*Never Dated*

Reading these comments, one can only begin to understand the suffering and sadness for those seeking love, left out of the spotlight. Voices of compassion add a sense of balance and care...

There are lots of individuals that have no social skills or confidence; they remain alone and unhappy. If they pay for the date then they at least have the confidence that when they show up at the meeting place the date won't snort and walk away. Everyone is looking to classify and compartmentalize people, actions, outcomes. If someone is afraid of something or can't wrap their brain around it, they go ahead and criticize it.

And...

Nothing will help these men more than spending time with what they feel are attractive women... If the women who sign up don't mind, and the men clearly don't mind, then leave them alone.

And...

I don't understand why people are in such a huff about all of this. Why does it matter that some men pay to get a date? It just makes the female that much more valuable. People need to stop judging others for their actions. As long as those people are happy doing what they do, then other people need to keep their comments to themselves.

Another poster asked, "Should people who can't get a date suffer?"

Should these people who have trouble getting dates due to being unattractive or socially inept just languish on the vine and never date? I think this site can be a good thing if used properly. I like that the owner will kick that guy off for using the site to solicit for sex.

Some commenters congratulated Wade...

This is the first time that I have not totally agreed with you, Anderson. I am a 66-year-old single woman who has been on at least five different dating websites. I stopped them all because it seemed that the only reason men were on these sites was to have sex. I think the gentleman on your show today who started this website should be congratulated. I would love to know that someone wanted to meet me enough to pay, with no expectation of getting laid, thereby truly having the opportunity, in a nice environment, to see if there is a connection.

And some, albeit speaking for a very select group, downright celebrated him...

I think Brandon Wade is a genius. I mean, think about it! If you are socially awkward, nearly 60 years old, and you're loaded as hell, eCompanion and the other dating websites are tough to use. Brandon Wade's website is extremely helpful for a socially awkward millionaire to use and to increase his self-confidence. Just listening to him talk today has really inspired me. I think he should continue speaking on behalf of his website's philosophy. Way to go, Brandon!

Several viewers, who clearly seem exhausted and disappointed by the sensationalist divisiveness that has taken over mass media news outlets such as this show, raised thoughtful objections, bemoaning a lost chance to dive deeper...

I found the show to be disappointing. It could have been an opportunity to discuss how our culture has evolved and is isolating us from one another. We may have widened our world, but we are increasingly disconnected. The idea of nerds getting assistance to meet others is a beneficial one in my opinion; so what if it costs money? Nerds can also be women, introverts, disabled, etc. To sensationalize what could be a positive service reminded me of cheap talk TV. If this is to be the tone of the show, I won't be watching.

And many voices simply brought a knowing, forgiving, experienced tone to the debate...

This site is no different from any other dating site, there are always people expecting sex on the first date and there are always prostitutes trolling around as well.

And…

I think the site is okay. You are only paying for the first date. You're not paying for sex, so it's not prostitution. That word was thrown around a lot during the show but we all know the meaning is sex for money and that's simply not happening with this site. The owner might need to work harder on weeding out the people that are trying to have sex for money… As long as nothing illegal is going on then nothing is wrong.

And…

I have been on a lot of dating sites for the last six years. So far all I have met are losers, liars, and lunatics. The free sites have the most lunatics on them. I am going to look into this site and see how it goes. They can't make me do anything I don't want to do and I am sick of being alone…

And…

I think the dating site owner is not responsible for

some subscribers' potential bad behavior. This site simply helps people (adults!) to meet and date—that's all. Whatever happens after the people meet are choices made by the adults involved, and bad behaviors are happening no matter how people meet... As for fees involved, dating sites like Match.com charge fees, which are for the site owners, while this site is designed to compensate women's time for dating. I think this guy is quite thoughtful. It is unfortunate that Anderson criticized the dating site owner the same way he criticized some dirty sites' owners, whose websites are doing nothing but damaging peoples' lives. I think they are very different in many ways. I liked Anderson's show until today. There was too much moral judgment from Anderson and the audience members. Today's target was simply wrong!

Wade found great solace in these comments. He welcomed the controversy of the episode, because, in the end, it only increased his exposure and populated the site further. And, again, good to his word, when one of the male members of WYP on the show admitted that he did, in fact, use it to make "indecent proposals" to women at the end of his dates, Wade pledged to kick him off the site.

And that's precisely what he did.

This Is Not An Online Brothel!

Despite the many reasons members register for WYP, because money is involved some people assume it's merely a front, merely a playground for hookers. That it's nothing more than a dark, seamy electronic alleyway for predatory men to buy needy women's sexual favors. It's got to be a scam site for good-looking girls, who have no intention to start an actual relationship, to deftly fleece lonely men for dinners—and garner a nice, fat cash bonus for their efforts. It can't be what it seems—simply a guy paying for the right to go on a first date with an attractive woman.

So what's true? What are people's experiences? Are there "gold-diggers" on this site? There are gold-diggers on every online dating site. Most populate places like Millionaire Match, Seeking Arrangement, or any site with the words "sugar daddy" in it. Might as well dig where the gold is buried. And on every site there are escorts seeking potential customers. It's not uncommon.

But it's the bald, unapologetic exchange of money that raises the particular specter of prostitution around WYP for many, because prostitution is the first frame of reference that they have. "Man gives woman money = prostitution." It's a familiar equation. But the truer frame here is "money exchange = a door opener," not unlike a salesman or doctor paying fees at a country club to gain access to its moneyed membership. Nevertheless, some people knee-jerkingly slot WYP as just another variety of hooking.

Rhonda is a highly educated secondary school teacher who has been enjoying WYP, and scoffs at those charges...

It's not prostitution. I'm sure there are escorts here, but the majority of people are using it exactly for what it's supposed to be. My time is valuable. I teach. I bring work home. I have my own personal business to take care of. If a man is going to break off some money for entertainment—why shouldn't it go to me? I'm more entertaining that most shows (laughs)—and we both might discover there's lasting chemistry.

Albert, a warm, thoughtful San Francisco PhD in his late 50s and a father of adult children in their twenties, agrees...

Prostitution? That's insulting! These are quality women on this site—plus there's a big banner on the home page that screams, "do not expect sex on the first date!" We are consenting adults, and I always ask for a phone number right away. If I don't hear back from her, forget it. If there is follow-up, we move on to a date. I have never had that expectation that sex was expected—and even if it were a sugar-daddy arrangement, I don't know anyone in their 40s who will provide sexual favors for 100 dollars!

The male members of the site show annoyance when they hear the site described as a hooker site. Admonishes one straight-talking black belt martial arts instructor who is seeking a life partner...

I would call it prostitution if you have sex, but if you're paying a lady for her time, for dinner, and you don't have sex, it's not prostitution. Straight and simple.

Rebecca, a celibate Christian author seeking a husband, agrees...

It's as far from prostitution as I can imagine. It's paying for someone's time—there's no defined sexual act being paid for. Anyone who says that is illiterate. I saw the Anderson Cooper Show when Brandon went on. And I thought, "Anderson, people—are you really this stupid?" Prostitution is an exchange of sex act for money—anything else is time-exchange for money. I felt bad for Brandon. They were ganging up on him and being unfair.

To prevent the site from devolving into a pay-for-play playground, Wade has taken numerous steps. First, there is that clear, written admonition on the home page that escorts are not allowed. No profile is allowed to suggest that sex is being offered or expected. Site guidelines instruct "no mention of sex" be included in the e-mail messaging back and forth once a potential date prospect is unlocked. Says Wade, "If they want escorts, there are other sites. You can write in your profile, 'I love sex,' but you can't say, 'I want sex.' Nevertheless, people are creative and for example, a woman might suggest in her profile that she would be very open to a very generous offer that included dinner 'and perhaps dessert'." Use your judgment," he tells users. "Be very clear about what you are asking for, what you want, and what you are getting into."

The ancient truth is that where there are money and men, there will be women who want to separate the two, and they will do almost anything to accomplish that. Some male members encountered this unexpectedly after opening conversations with attractive members. Said one bemused member...

I came across a couple of escorts. They will pretty much tell you after they get your phone number what they want. They'll be straightforward. Hell, they're in business, so they should be! To tell you the truth, they'll come to your house for a couple hundred bucks anyway and you can find them on a thousand sites so there's no point in using this site for that.

And conversely, wherever there are attractive women, there will appear men who will offer money for sexual favors. Says Sonia, a member from Miami...

On Match.com—guys, they all expect the same: sex for free. I don't have that problem on this site because I know how to say no. I tell them in my profile and in our first conversations that I am assuming you are a gentleman, we can have dinner and a conversation, and if we have chemistry, we can have 2nd date...

It goes without saying that the ability to say "no" to an offer, "no" during conversations, and "no" during dinner to anything beyond the first date are options every woman has on the site. Which makes the charge of "prostitution" absurd to many of the members, if not outright offensive.

Prostitution? They don't know what they are talking about. I don't go out with just anybody. WYP's actually similar to Match.com for me, because I only go out with men I think I may truly consider as a partner. The only difference is, we

agree on an amount and, at least I'm not wasting my time. It's just Match with a time guarantee.
—*Laurie, Pharma Rep, 35*

Men who are serious about meeting a high-quality life partner can also filter out who they don't want—for instance the women looking for a quick buck. Says one member from the Midwest...

I'll go up to $200 for a genuine, classy, accomplished and beautiful woman. Some want $500 and they can bite me—they're former Playboy models and stuff like that. I weed them out quickly.

Caveat emptor, here as always.

Self-Selection and the Women of WYP

Online dating sites tend to be self-selecting. eHarmony, though its vaunted "scientific" algorithm has been debunked by most reputable sources (including *Scientific American Mind* magazine), nevertheless is good hunting grounds for a more traditional wife or husband—simply because people who are *seeking* a spouse tend to register on eHarmony.

Sugar daddies and sugar babies go to sites that have the word "sugar" or "millionaire" in them, along with sites like SeekingArrangement.com. Jewish people often use JDate.com as their primary site, religious Christians use ChristianMingle.com, and most canny people will often post a second profile on OKCupid.com and PlentyofFish.com. Those two are free and are rather like the pit in Shakespeare's Globe Theater, where the masses gathered and jostled.

According to founder Brandon Wade, WYP tends to attract more "independent thinkers"...

The money exchange, though innocent enough, feels "naughty". Because the concept of the site is still socially unacceptable, the fact that a man or woman goes on this site says right away that he or she is a more independent thinker, that they are more out of the box, willing to do something naughty, even racy. They'll give something new a shot.

Gary is a powerhouse attorney in Los Angeles, and agrees that WYP draws more out-of-the-box types of members...

When you add the element of money, you draw on a different crowd of women. Everybody knows this is not a conventional meet at a bar or through friends—that dramatically changes their open-mindedness—no usual rules. For someone like me— I've been married, got kids, I'm not looking to meet someone who has a set timeline for me. Most of the girls I meet socially are on a timeline. Here, no one says we're gonna date for a few months then talk about kids and marriage. I have time constraints— so I tell them that our time should feel more like vacation time. I've got kids—four kids! The women I date understand that about me from the start! I am clear I don't have tons of spare time. On this site— they are much more respectful of my time. On other sites, they ask for more and more time.

That set of expectations is changed right off the bat. It's self-selection. Women know I've got kids. Women in their late 20s won't be wondering that first night if I'm gonna be the one. Even if not overtly on the first date but by the third or by the time I see her naked—they won't start asking—where is this going? On this site—unlike everywhere else—women are not like that. They're fair. They're not afraid to ask what's going on with my life, what am I looking for. There's a lot of self-exploration and exploration of each other's lives on WYP.

The second part of what makes this site different is that girls don't feel like they're being taken advantage of. They feel more like they are taking advantage of me! I'm clear about it—I give money when I sit down. I will hand you the money when we sit and you can get up and walk away if you want—it's entirely in their hands. No pressure. I don't want to be with you if you don't want to hang out with me. I am VERY clear that there are no expectations. The women who come to this site seem to like that. They are independent and straight-shooters. Not your normal girl.

Jackie, a 36-year-old researcher in the Boston area, wears her independent mindset as a badge of honor...

I love the site! I tell my judgmental friends— you're cowards, you don't trust yourselves. You are afraid to follow something without a script. WYP is innovative, it's new. There are no rules. You have to make it up as you go. And the fact is, I'm having a really good time. Bottom line—I'm having a blast! Every week or so, I end up going out with someone new who I'd never meet, otherwise. It's a wild card—they just thought it was good opportunity to get a one-on-one moment to prove himself a candidate for a potentially great marriage with a great woman.

Shelley is a behavioral specialist in Philly who understands that there are good men who need that first leg up, or need an introduction. She is less interested in a man's outer trappings "than in his heart." She wants one thing: marriage. And to a good, smart, independent-minded man. That's why What's Your Price captured her imagination.

There's tons of competition out there! Men know that they would get lost in the crowd if they didn't get this chance to show themselves for who they are. I treat them with respect for taking that chance—for being a risk-taker. I give them the benefit of the doubt that anyone who's on this site is an out-of-the-box thinker. I assume you have the highest motivation and let's see if we can create something awesome in the moment...

Almost by contrast, the site also tends to attract "traditionalists" or those who like "old fashioned" values. Despite years of advancing equalization in the workplace and new social expectations of respect, many women still like men who open doors and who are, in traditional ways, powerful, or protective.

Sonia is an Argentinean, whose wealthy fiancé died suddenly. She relocated to the States and tried online dating to begin her life over...

> *I started with Match. It was not a terrible experience. There are liars like everywhere. I did meet someone very nice and we dated a bit. But the men on WYP are different, a different type of man, more professional. On Match, younger men wrote me, which was flattering for a while, but I like men older than me because I like to respect my man. The men here are different because they have their own companies, they say they are looking for love, though I'm not so sure everyone's looking for lasting love.*

Nadia is another import from a more traditional culture. She came to the U.S. from the former Yugoslavia seeking fortune, fame, and, of course, love, not necessarily in that order. She is a well-placed a multimedia journalist covering the high-end entertainment business in New York City and has been on *What's Your Price* since summer 2011, and adores it. "I'm meeting the kind of men I want to meet: chivalrous gentlemen." Every one of the ten men Nadia has dated arrived on time, took her out for a lovely dinner, did not proposition her for sex, and paid for everything, including her $100 agreed-upon offer, without any fuss.

I like the kind of guy who likes to take care of a girl. In a relationship, I want the type who'll be man of the house and take care of things. With WYP you know, because of the payment, they're more likely to want to take care of women. On the others you can't tell what they're looking for in a relationship.

It should be noted that Nadia has succeeded in finding appropriate dates because she knows herself well, knows what she wants, reads men's profiles carefully, and only dates men who fit the guidelines she's developed. Though she had only two second-dates, she says it's been a matter of a lack to the intensity of chemistry she is seeking. And she remains optimistic about future prospects.

Nadia's offers have averaged $100 each. She loves being paid for first dates...

In this city, dating is an everyday thing. It can be expensive and sometimes a waste of time. All the money I spend on cab fare, makeup, mani and pedicure, just for two hours with someone I might not even like. Now at least I'm not wasting cab fare.

She rejected a man who offered her $20 and thinks the low-ballers don't really like the WYP system. "They seem like they're not really comfortable with the site," she says. "They ask me if I think it's the right way to do things, or they ask other questions that make me uncomfortable. If they don't like it, why are they on it? I didn't go out with any guys who acted like that."

Curiously, Nadia has never tried other dating websites, and is so suspicious of them she won't...

> *A male friend of mine is on Match.com, and he says he loves it because "he gets laid 3 or 4 times a week. When I heard that I thought, for sure I'm not going there! Women are more vulnerable on those websites—they think guys are looking for relationships, but all they want is sex.*

Nadia intends to keep trying to find someone on WYP, someone:

> *[W]ho is comfortable being a man and taking care of a woman; someone who likes to take responsibility. He has to be financially stable, and not stingy. Where I come from men are supposed to take care of women, so that is my mentality. I can take care of myself by myself, but with a*

partner I want to be treated like a lady. I don't want to take care of him.

Tracy is in her early 20s, a religious girl who values traditional behaviors and going slow. She has dated several men on WYP and, despite the fact that one of them lied to her and was married (she declined the second date), she finds that the men are more "mature" on this site than elsewhere...

The men are more respectful and generous. They are willing to pay to show that they are genuine about getting to know you. I like older guys. They are more mature. Since most of them have good jobs, and are used to being in a workplace and a position of authority, they are used to being respectful to others. They're more friendly. A lot of them are successful so all they want to do on a date is relax and have fun. It's never boring. They're more comfortable with themselves. On POF, all the guys wanted was sex. They didn't have any money so were always covering up or rushing things or making excuses.

Because the perception is that men on the site have a little more cash than men on other sites (but really, what is another $50 or $100 dollars for a date?), women who prefer more traditional male/female dynamics register. From many of their stories, you can hear a lot of frustration with what David M. Granger, the editor of *Esquire* magazine, has often described as the "extended adolescence of the American male." As one woman's profile laid it out...

> *Why I am here? I'm tired of Peter Pans, baby boys, and changing diapers. I like men, real men that know how to treat a true woman like me. I am not picky but I am selective when it comes to the quality of people I have a connection with. I am allergic to drama and mind games. I prefer honesty even when it's the brutal truth, but at least you know what the other person stands for. I strive to be a life enhancer and I enjoy to see that in others.*

What's curious is that of the many women I spoke with, almost no one came in with stars in her eyes. Efficiency, a mercantile practicality, and a sense of being valued by men for their time were the most common themes sounded. Rebecca, the 35-year-old writer, sounded all three...

> *I like this site—I'm the "it" girl—accomplished, vital, successful, healthy, attractive—and at this point it's hard to get a date with me at all. I have high standards intellectually and physically plus I*

have a three year old, so I'm not going to take a risk with my time. I don't want to take unnecessary time away from my three year old, so if I feel like I'm getting the wage I'm accustomed for my time—it takes the risk out. It gives a guy to get a chance to say okay, here I am, this is who I am. Without the site, he never would have had a chance and believe me, I'm all ears. I want a good man in my life.

Another constituency is the highly attractive woman taking refuge from being approached, addressed, and even assaulted by every man out there in the big, bad world. As a man, I have experienced this constant verbal and non-verbal barrage when walking through a crowd with a beautiful woman on my arm. If eyes were arrows, she'd be St. Sebastian a thousand times over. For these women, in essence, WYP functions as a bomb shelter.

If you're attractive online, you get bombarded day and night. Jolene is a bright brunette with a design background. She's also high-cheekboned, doe-eyed, unintentionally sultry…

After I broke up with my boyfriend of five years, I just wanted to start over. I went on Match and put up a profile. When I came home from work that day I had over 200 e-mails! Some were gross. Most of the guys clearly didn't even read my profile. I felt cheapened—no, assaulted! I couldn't even get through them all...

If you happen to be a beautiful woman, you get bombed on the other dating sites. Bombed by e-mails from every man who pays his thirty bucks a month, or nothing, in the case of OKCupid and Plenty of Fish. On those sites, online dating is a free pass to stuff the unguarded inboxes of beautiful women. For many men, it's as if the force-field around attractive women has dropped temporarily and so they fire away. They write without serious intent of getting a date. They write the way propaganda planes drop leaflets over crowded squares. They write as Hail-Mary passes. They write to salve themselves, to feel the tingle of connection, unrequited as it may be. They write to see if they can wangle a quick fuck on the chance they might entice a lonely broad on an off night. And they write to kill time. And feeling.

The guys who wink at me on Match—I would ask "really?" I'm not a model or anything but I'm a tall, attractive, slim woman and they were short, fat, bald, old and unemployed—but come on, give me a break.

—Annie, 37, Event Planner

Gina is an accomplished woman in her late thirties,

who calls herself a classy redhead. She came to What's Your Price because…

I figured I'd meet a different genre of people on this site. New men, men who might move in circles I've missed where I live. On the other sites, if you live outside one of the major cities, you just see the same old people over and over.

And she's been happy…

I've been on 8 dates… okay, one guy was married. I've been out with super-nice guys, classy. In fact, one was the best date I've ever had online, but I had just met someone else. I like the control I have on WYP. I don't go out with a guy I'm not attracted to at all, even if he offered $1,000. Actually, especially if he offered $1,000 because I would wonder what he really wanted. I only go out with the guys I would go out with anyway. I have only kissed one guy—who I really liked. I liked them all, though. They were all nice, classy—true gentlemen.

Clarissa is an artist, an avant-garde dancer and out-of-the box thinker…

On other sites, every kind of guy in the world

wrote me, even though I said I like creative types. I got truckers, accountants, blue-collar types. They all just wrote me because, I suppose, they thought I was pretty, and besides, why the hell not? It doesn't cost them anything to shoot off a letter to a pretty young thing. On WYP, they are a different kind of man, plus they are spending not only money but credits on the site to get a date, so I assume from the start they really mean it. The guys are more willing to be a little adventurous, more spontaneous, more generous. Just a different category.

The common theme of feeling valued for their time directly contradicts the impulse to believe that "buying" a date somehow demeans women. Many women admit that the process restores their sense of dignity. WYP functions as an important filter. Says Leanne, a 37-year-old Chicagoan...

WYP filters out the flakes, which takes care of the bottom rung of my concerns. For me, Match.com was a nightmare. Every day, I was attracting men who live with their mommies! Seriously, I began to worry that this was my level, that this was what was natural for me. I got really depressed. When I joined WYP, I was suddenly getting date offers from professionals, from business owners—

real men with real lives—and real houses and apartments of their own.

The letter-bombing of pretty women on the popular dating sites doesn't serve men, either. When women's e-mail boxes get flooded with quarter-hearted offers, it drowns out the voices of the men who genuinely want to make a connection. Says Doug, a single father and MBA entrepreneur who owns five businesses:

> *On other sites, I never had time or patience for all that back-and-forth which goes nowhere. Even after all that nonsense, I never went on a single date! There are too many nudniks going after too few girls...*

As with almost everything on the Internet, the task is to stand out from all the white noise. A fantastic profile may do it. Cash can, too. Gary is a successful, handsome, busy tech exec and active father of one in Southern California...

> *I'm no sugar daddy, so at first, I thought this site was cheesy. But after trying it out for a couple of days, I saw the value for someone like me. I have expendable cash—and I saw that WYP very quickly weeds out the scrubs. In normal date conversation, I ask women why they chose this*

site and they almost to-the-one said that guys on other dating sites message-bomb girls. By bidding on a date, it makes you stand out more—which solves the problem I had with the other dating sites.

Plus, because the pool is smaller, and because women are more incentivized to write to men first, the whole contacting and meeting process gets accelerated. Doug adds...

It was easier to start communicating with a good-looking woman. Girls don't get a lot of scrubs bombarding them—and it's an interesting dynamic. The girls reach out to you, which I never had before, and I like.

BIG, a 52-year-old securities manager living in Atlanta, Georgia, has gone out with 37 women since joining *WYP*. He's tried five other dating sites and has been making the romantic rounds online since the breakup of his second marriage four years ago, giving him an eagle's view of online dating. WYP is, he says, "a fabulous concept", especially when compared to more general sites.

My profile [on Match.com] has been viewed 631 times, I've sent over 300 messages, and I have had exactly one date. On WYP I had a date within three days of joining. It's the law of supply and demand: there's a limited supply of beautiful women, and they're in high demand. On most sites women are bombarded with so many e-mails they have no incentive to respond to all of them. On WYP they have an incentive, so the average guy has a better chance.

I discovered another curious reversal of expectations. Whereas for many people, their first reaction to a woman taking money for a date makes her suspect, mercenary, or lascivious, the self-valuing that comes with graciously accepting a cash offering for a dinner date actually raises the status of women in some men's eyes. Says one member, who is seeking his second wife after having had a long first marriage…

I like the self-confidence of a woman who can stand up and say, "Sure, I'll go on a date for $100 or $150." There's a fear that men have that women just want the money or the free lunch— but that's why it's important to screen them.
—Albert, 56

Quality does not only mean money on WYP, although the money exchange would seem to suggest that. Some women find it hard to find men on the open market because they are attractively intelligent, and thereby "place out" of the popular dating arenas. Just as there are awkward nerd men with beautiful hearts who can't get the attention of attractive women, so are there gifted, attractive women who can't get the attention of the nerds they adore. Rebecca, 35, lives just outside L.A.

I heard about WYP on my newsfeed. In the 80s, I did a study on people who use classified ads to meet people. I was trying to dispel the negative stigma of it. My research showed what I suspected, that people were too busy, looking for an efficient way to make maximum number of dates with minimum time trolling ads. They wanted to prescreen. Time and efficiency were the main reason they used classified ads. Not trolling for sex, which was the popular idea back then...

As a social psych major—I saw Brandon on a news show—and I saw how this could work with shy, socially awkward men. Wow, I thought. Helping nerds make contact with an attractive women! I was all in—I'm a nerd disguised as an attractive woman. I like academic, really techy people, but they won't ask me out! I'll flirt and smile and put myself out there and they won't even try asking me out. I'm a real hanky-dropper! But either they are intimidated by my looks and eliminate themselves as an option, or their needs to be an introductory process put into place. Smart guys look at me and think they have no chance—but I'm practically screaming, "try me!" It's a reverse prejudice. They make assumptions because I'm hot. They don't know what I want...

WYP sounded perfect for me. I'm interested in an accomplished person who won't be freaked out that I read and love science, but I'm hot, too. It's a crazy thing—my looks have been an obstacle to meeting men—dumb jocks will ask me out, but in three seconds I know we'd have nothing in common. The guys who I like are not pumping themselves up in the gym, they are out there thinking about making contribution to society...

Rebecca has had good luck on the site. She took a few dates at $200, then noticed a profile that caught her attention...

Then I met a guy who had funny, quirky stuff on his profile that would make it hard for him to find a date. But he was real—I could see his heart. We are still dating, still see each other three times a week and it's going well. He'll take me grocery shopping, never lets me pay for anything. I don't take advantage. He's obsessed with film noir, he will launch into lectures, his diction and vocabulary are unusual—a real nerd!—but he has a heart of gold and is emotionally intelligent. We both are Christians, and having a Christian courtship—celibate. We kind of kiss. He wants a wife and kids so we are taking this seriously, one step at a time.

Celibacy. Film noir. A nerd love story. The experiment unfolds...

Dollars and Sense: This is How We Hedge Our Bets

"I never thought I'd be on a site like this, but I just
got really tired of wasting time, money, and energy
getting ready for dates (hair, make-up, nails,
new dress, etc.) with men who were late,
flaked at the last minute, left me with the
bill or just weren't worth it, in general."

—From a WYP Profile,
Attractive Woman, age 31

Dating is expensive. If you're a man and you live in a major metro area, and you take a woman out for dinner, it's going to run you between $50–$150 dollars. With wine, drinks, and dessert, that number can easily double.

Is a promising woman worth that for a date? Sure. But what if, as a man, you want to date several different women, either because that's your taste or because you are working hard to find the right one to pursue for a long-term relationship or marriage? Three dates a week can get you toward $500 dollars per week, which translates to $24,000 a year.

Now, if you're in your twenties, you're out at the bars and clubs, you're meeting each other socially, easily. There's no expectation of quiet romantic dinners. To daters in their twenties, that seems so "thirty"...or worse, "sixty". When you're 24, what's the difference? Thirty might as well be sixty.

But if you're a man in your thirties, or forties or beyond, the club scene becomes less of an option. Chances are, you work longer hours. Chances are, you need to schedule your time more carefully, be less spontaneous, and are compelled to set a "date" for certain evenings if you want to get to know a certain lady. There are fewer gray areas in your life, less wiggle room, given work hours, gym time, taking care of your food, your dry cleaning, and all the daily responsibilities of adult life. Add children from a previous marriage into the mix and suddenly, single nightlife begins to sound prohibitively expensive. Do you really want to hit the bars, dropping money for drink after drink, hoping to strike up a conversation? Or would you rather guarantee a first date with a woman you find attractive, for the cost of a few drinks?

The search for love and intimate companionship can be expensive for men. But, in some ways, it is worse for women. In a financial column, writer Jessica Bosari names grooming one of the top five budgetary expenses for women.

Whether it is for professional or personal reasons, it typically cost(s) more for women to maintain presentable appearances. Hair care, nail care, and other cosmetic expenses can add up in the long run."

Indeed, in a March, 2011 survey, 65% of women said they spent more than $50 preparing for a single date. This may come as a shocker for most men, who see only the bill being dropped by waiters to their side of the table.

For male readers, let's look at a hypothetical date scenario. Three days from now Gina is going out to dinner with Justin, whom she met several weeks ago for the first time, online. She'll need someone to stay with her daughter Kelsey, so, after four calls, she finally locates a girl who's available. First expense:

Babysitter: 4 hours @ $10 per = $40.00

The next morning, Gina notices her toenail polish is chipped and callouses have formed on the soles of her feet. Justin's taking her to a nice place and she wants to wear strappy heels. It's been two months since her last pedicure, and with work and all, she doesn't have time to do them herself. So she asks the babysitter to come an hour early on date night and books the salon.

Extra hour babysitter: $10.00
Pedicure: $20.00
Pedicure with Manicure: $35.00

Having put off the expense as long as possible, Gina drops her favorite "first date" dress at the dry-cleaners...

Dry cleaning: $10.00

Then there's hair. One night, after tucking her daughter into bed, Gina highlights her dark brown hair. She tries to take care of it herself, but it's been a while since she's been for a cut. She examines herself. She's not twenty-five anymore. She really likes Justin. She noticed he's a good dresser and she wants to make her best impression. She schedules a time with her haircutter.

Henna: $9.99
Professional cut and highlighting: $125.00

So to review:

Cost of Date:
Babysitter, 5 hours:	$50
Dry cleaning:	$10
Pedicure:	$20
Henna:	$10
Hair:	$125
Total	$215

Now, this tabulation may not be news to women readers but to men, it's a revelation. We want our dates to look top form but don't really think about what goes into it. We want to feel proud sitting with our woman, or walking into a restaurant. We want to be refreshed and inspired by her beauty. But at the same time, most men fantasize about what she looks like that the moment she opens her eyes in the morning. And that's to say nothing of the cost of transportation back and forth to the date, clothing, parking, valet, gas, etc.— things we may take for granted.

So the $215 dollars may be a shocker. Now, gentlemen, let me kick this up a whopper of a notch. If you want to really have a heart attack, try walking into a Sephora shop, or take a slow stroll through the make-up department of a Bloomingdales or Nordstrom one afternoon.

But let me warn you. Bring a calculator and get ready to add. Eyebrow pencil, eyeliner, mascara, foundation, powder, blush, lipstick, lip-liner, perfume. Try to find a bottle or tube of anything under $30 dollars. There are concoctions to be found on these shelves that seem as exotic and mysterious as potions from a witch's lair... bronzer, primer, high-definition foundation (yes, that's foundation in HD, whatever that means), concealer, glycolic acid, toner, caviar creams, 24-carat gold leaf facials, night creams, day creams, de-puffing eye balms, pore-minimizers, laser-free resurfacing kits, firming lotions, lift gels, exfoliators, resurfacers, scruffing lotion (wtf?), "refined finish facial polish", mud masks, sulfur masks, eye masks, brushes, and eye of newt. Okay, maybe no eye of newt, but wait a few months. You never know what the next "must-have" trend will be.

The bottom line: beauty isn't cheap, and both we and the women we date want them to feel and look their best. What do we do to get ready for a date? Well, speaking for myself, a fresh change of a shirt, which I keep in my car, a wash of my face and hands and spritz of cologne perhaps that I keep in the trunk with the spare engine oil and jack kit, and I'm ready to go.

Men are generally oblivious to what women go through—and pay—to get ready for a date. For example, on the Bravo show *The Millionaire Matchmaker,* one suitor arranged, as a first date, a swimming session before lunch, and was angry when the woman refused to go in the water. What he didn't realize was that she'd spent all morning working on her makeup and hair, and wasn't about to destroy it in a second, then go to lunch looking like a wet poodle. "Does he think I looked this way when I rolled out of bed?" she asked rhetorically.

Some women have decided to take this education of men into their own hands. One woman wrote in a *WYP* online discussion forum that she likes taking a date to a spa early on, because...

It gives a man the full picture of how much beauty treatments cost. The total for a massage, hair, facial micropeel, body wrap, and eyelash extensions comes to $900.00. Most guys' jaws drop. Welcome to my world!

Some men already get it, and it factors into their feeling that WYP answers a natural need. Albert is a soft-voiced business owner who also happens to be a PhD and adventure travel enthusiast. He's 56, and understands the economics of looking good, and, in turn, the innovation of WYP.

I like the concept as it's [elucidated]. A woman will put out a lot of time and energy getting ready for a date, and I don't mind compensating her for it. Also, let's face it, women understand that a hundred bucks doesn't equal a whole week of meals. It won't be her "living"...

Figuring in all the expenses a woman has to go through to look fabulous for a date, one begins to see the practical allure for her of being compensated for her time. Wrote one woman on the WYP blog:

We're only getting money for the first date, so $50 isn't enough to cover everything. My spray tan alone costs that much, not to mention freshly *done toes and nails. My lotions and potions are also expensive. I go all-out for a date; I'd feel weird without my war paint.*

Says Ariel, who lives in Denver:

I couldn't fall in love with a poor man. I wasn't always this heartless—as a teenager I used to fall in love with underprivileged boys. Then I got practical.

In an ideal world, men and women would make the same amount of money, and the green stuff would never come into the picture. But here in the real world, the world in which we live, women still only earn 77 cents to the dollar that men make. Is that an improvement from 1970, when women earned only 51 cents to the male dollar? Sure. But are things even? Not yet. Which also means, incidentally, that $100 spent on dating by a woman is proportionally more than that same $100 by a man. With the recent publication of Liza Mundy's book *The Richer Sex: How the New Majority of Female Breadwinners Is Transforming Sex, Love and Family,* trends seem to be skewing strongly toward women making even more money than men in the next generation—but it's not true yet. Perhaps the columns will start tipping at that point, with more "generous" women dating "attractive" men.

For many a woman, men paying for a date represents "tangible respect" for her time and trouble for preparing for a date. Some say that the additional bid for the pleasure of her company represents an additional marker of his respect. As we will see in the next chapter, for the men on the site, paying for her time gives him a warm, traditional sense of "taking care of" a women. For others, the cash payment is simply practical: a valued shortcut.

Buying A Spot At The Front of the Line: Here Come The Men

Just as for the eager job seekers Wade saw scrambling for rare jobs in the post-bubble economy in San Francisco, in the dating arena, there is a scattered army of men clambering to meet a limited number of attractive women. And because there are attractive women who have the self-esteem (or financial incentive) to say, "Hey, I'm worth $100–$200 for you to try to win my heart"—men have been registering in droves on What's Your Price. What's fascinating is how many different kinds of men sign up, and for how many reasons.

As mentioned earlier, WYP offers an "old-fashioned" feel for men who like the old ways, before women earned a fairer wage and were expected to pay for things. Comments Sandra, an event coordinator from a mid-sized city...

It attracts the kind of men who like to be a gentleman, who like to take charge, they know what they want, they are powerful—honestly, believe it or not, there are more of that type of man here on this site than others.

You could say that WYP lends respect to a certain kind of man, the kind of man who feels more worthwhile when he can express his appreciation by paying for an evening with a woman. In the hurly-burly of popular culture, guys like this take a lot of abuse. When Wade appeared on the popular Tom Lykis radio show, he was derided viciously for the WYP formula. "Why should I pay for a date?" the guys screamed over the line. "Let her buy me a drink!" In the popular conception, these abrasive "bad-boys" get the girls.

But the truth is, there are many women who have a soft spot for the kind of guy who is quieter, more gracious, who has what we used to call "manners". Says Lisa, a pastry chef in San Diego:

> *I'm on this site because I used to like the guys in high school who stood along the wall at school dances. Who were in rocketry club. Who couldn't believe their luck that I would come over and talk to them. They are cute to me—and you know what, they treat me nicer!*

Men may feel ashamed about being "old-fashioned" in a world of slickster pick-up artists with their canned witticisms and pointy shoes, but on WYP, they find a more welcoming home. Heather (as you might tell from her language) is a young techie in the Bay Area...

OKCupid is good if you want to parse down your lifestyle particularities, like if you're bisexual. There are a lot of questions you have to fill out— to determine your peccadilloes—how straight you are, how experimental. It's a good way to refine. They create a huge database with a good search system and it's good for finding sexual specifics. WYP is better for me because my main goal is to find one very smart, very nerdy, and more traditional guy. They tend to come to this site because they find it hard to break through the noise of the bigger, more general sites, where a big Mitt Romney smile and full head of hair opens doors.

In this way, WYP tends to self-select for women who respect the kind of quiet, even awkward, more traditional man who likes to take care of a woman. In many interviews with women, the word "gentleman" often comes up. Leanne, 38, runs a retail shop in a moneyed town in Connecticut:

There was this one guy, he was older, heavier. His profile was charming and he was clearly a gentleman. Honestly, I would never have gone out with him otherwise, but because he paid, I went. It ended up we had good chemistry. Trust me, I would never have met him otherwise. But we fell for each other. After a few dates, we had sex—but it was the best sex I ever had in my life! He was really in tune with the woman's body—and he could meet my needs. I'm still seeing him. I don't know if he's really going to be my "guy" but so far, it's been beautiful.

In many ways, this is an "old-fashioned" quality. But it is also "old country". Sonia moved to the US from Buenos Aires.

I'm so surprised that I found this site in this country—this is the first site for getting paid for a date. In my country, we don't have that, but I am personally trained by my ex to be treated like that. Money is just a way of showing that a man cares for a woman—I'm not wasting my time, my hair, my makeup, by best perfumes on just anyone. I am a lady—I am from a country where the gentleman is the provider—I need to admire the man—he needs to be more successful than me.

Another significant category of men on the site includes the business owners and hardworking office warriors mentioned earlier. The relaxed, casual socializing of college and early adulthood are luxuries long gone. Gary owns a small tech business and finds himself shuttling among California's major cities several times a week.

When I show up for our date, women ask me, "Why is such a good-looking guy here?" And I tell them the truth—I'm too busy to meet women any other way. I mean specifically, attractive women, the kind I would consider for a girlfriend or wife. I honesty don't meet that many women on a day-to-day basis. I consider it actually to be my greatest personal challenge. I'm in tech and I'm with guys all day, everywhere I go.

Gary is a high-powered property attorney in Santa Monica. For him, WYP has been a godsend:

In my regular world, the people I meet are dorky lawyers like me. I can go on Match or Chemistry— it's a meat market—so formulaic—it's a waste of time—I lose interest in an hour. I don't have time to scroll through a thousand profiles...

The difference with WYP is that girls are very interested in meeting guys, they're not dabbling but pursuing. Which makes it easy for me to not pay much attention to it and still get dates. I have a busy practice plus kids of my own. I'm willing to pay for face time. Dinner's gonna be $200 anyway, what's another $100? It's the cost of admission. It's *worth it to see if I like someone and if they like me. I like that there's no time for dabbling and the whole dance. I tell them straight—we're going to see if there's chemistry and decide whether to have a second date.*

And with the divorce rate so high, there is a growing subset of busy businessmen who not only find it hard to meet attractive women during their daily rounds, but who also, frankly, need the "healing" experience of going on a few dates to get their groove back. WYP, which is designed to facilitate a smooth and swift passage to an actual sit-down date, is ideally suited for this. Rae is a beautician in the DC area...

I had one great date with a gentleman that had just been divorced. He had not dated for over 20 years and was nervous about it. He told me the process of bidding for a date gave him a level of security, because he knew the attraction was primarily the money... He knew that I was not going to expect a relationship, and that sex was not going to happen. He was glad that aspect was taken out of the equation because he was not ready for that yet. He just wanted to sit with a pretty girl like me and have a nice normal date again. It was sweet.

Angie is an astute observer of male-female dynamics from her apartment in lower Manhattan. She takes a similar, compassionate view of men's search for women…

Men want more than sex, beyond sex—they just want to be treated with kindness. Men are so burned out on being bitched at, criticized, condemned, ridiculed, yelled at, treated with disrespect—they are just aching to be with a lady who is kind. If something miraculous happens and he can make love to that woman, all the better. But every man I have met on WYP, it's clear to me that this is what he is hoping for: just to be treated with kindness. And they will pay anything they can afford just not be treated meanly. And it's wonderful as a woman to be able to treat a man with respect, take his arm, and proudly go where he wants to and let him tell his stories and appreciate him. Most women—I am embarrassed about them. I hate the way they talk about men—they are man-hating, they are man-bashing—I refuse to let them speak that way about men in my presence. I'll actually stop them. Like, they're angry because men want sex. Hey— men are hard-wired to have sex! If they're not running about raping people—leave them alone! I mean, thank god he wants to have sex! Most men want sex but also to make their lives better, and I wish women would pay more attention to that. Even with my best friends, who are smart and accomplished—they can be total bitches when it comes to men. If I were a man I would never get within three feet of some of them.

Halle is 29, working on an advanced degree and has dated about twelve men on WYP. She is also buxom and sassy and, frankly, a bombshell. She tells this story as matter of fact as if it happens every day...

I've never had a problem with a guy on this site. It's always been dinner first, to see if we, you know, connect. This one time, I met a guy—he asked to meet at the St Regis hotel. He meets me in the lobby but instead of going to dinner, he wants to get a room for our first date. I was suspicious of course, but he offers me $800 dollars just to come up and he's clear that he has no expectations. And all we did was talk for fifteen minutes. He just wanted to tell me what he was doing, how well he was doing in business, how much he loved it. He just wanted someone to talk to him. And then we went downstairs, had dinner and I went home. I've seen him at NBA games, down on the floor or up in the boxes. He's always with other people and I keep seeing him in *different places and we nod to each other. He's very polite.*

Getting back into romance can be a bumpy ride, to say the least. Paul is a highly-placed Bay Street financial guy in Toronto. He's had a tough decade, raising his daughter single-handedly, after his wife disappeared, and only recently stepped back into dating, now that his daughter is off to college. And he has found that the open seas of the dating world have been choppy...

I am late 40s, decent-looking and fit. I am not crazy nor do I have any really bad habits. So when I dove into dating again, I just wanted someone easygoing and normal. I went on OkCupid. My first date, she said she had an athletic build—yeah, she weighed 340—she was athletic like the center of the Giants offensive line is athletic.

The second woman said she'd come out and meet me. It was 10 p.m. I said, but didn't you write that you have kids 3 and 6?' She said she'd leave them in front of the TV. When I did meet with her, I knew I shouldn't, but I was new at this, she spent the whole time bitching about her ex-husband not sending payments. The next night I get some incoherent text about her wearing matching bra and panties—and could I send her 300 bucks!

The third girl I met on OkCupid got piss-drunk and asked me to chew through her stockings. Then she passed out.

I looked at Zoosk because they barrage me with offers through e-mail. They have this come-on— "Hey Paul! Guess what! Someone looked at your profile!" Now I have to pay just to see her. I got nowhere with this site. Now I can't figure out how to get off Zoosk. Someone tell me how!

One day, I read about WYP in The Globe and Mail—*the big Toronto paper. I thought, I'll give it a try. Fifty bucks for a date. I'm easy for fifty bucks and I could always run away. My first date, she was fifteen years younger, classy, articulate. We had a beer and wonderful time chatting.*

The dollar amount makes it easier—everything's up front. It's above-board and everywhere knows where everyone stands.

But the best part of this site is that the women write me. They are incentivized to write me here. On other sites, they would never write back, even when I sent them my one-of-a-kind charming letters. I like that they are approaching me here. I love the idea someone can wink at me and I can say, sure, fifty bucks, let's have a drink together. It's hard to take a woman out for less than fifty bucks anyway. But if I offer $50 and they come back and say $200, I pass."

This ability for good men to cut through the white noise of online dating and shortcut their way to meet real women, in the flesh, has been one of the most gratifying aspects of WYP for founder Brandon Wade.

WYP differs from other matchmaking sites, most of which operate haphazardly. For instance, on a first visit to a dating website, men often get dazzled by the sheer number of available attractive women, and sometimes go into a kind of trance or altered state, clicking madly and hitting on every enticing profile they see. On WYP, however, they have to assign a monetary value to each date, so they're forced to be more selective. They have to slow down and think about what they're doing, and can choose only those matches that genuinely suit them, rather than every beautiful babe that lights up the screen. Every man on WYP that I've spoken to has told me the same exact story: on other sites he'd reach out to hundreds of women, and hear back from one or two; on WYP he'd get, at minimum, a 50% response rate. On other sites he'd waste hours in fruitless pursuit.

Another single father, let's call him MOR after his profile name, says that though he's registered for several other online dating sites, he's not motivated to actually date anyone except from *WYP*.

> *It seems like everybody is lying on those sites, like Match.com and JDate. And the women are so jaded, a guy really has to work it to get their attention. I'd rather not spend time chasing after someone 5,000 other guys are chasing.*

He doesn't have much time to date, and not even for much of a relationship, as most of his home time is devoted to his three daughters. He just wants to go on some dates, enjoy the company of an attractive woman, relax, connect deeply perhaps, and feel good about himself.

> *When my daughters go off to college I'll probably want a long-term relationship again, but for now I just want to date. On WYP, I never have to face a Saturday night alone.*

Which brings us to another category of men I was interested to discover on the site—not the nerdy, not the older guys seeking younger girls, not the overworked—but simply the lonely. There are plenty of men who are aching for female company, not sex, just company, men who are not seeking "pay-for-play", but only to feel the warmth of a woman's smile, take a heady draught of a woman's sweet perfume, and feel like he is, once again, a valued member of the human race. Rae, who is one of the flashier girls on the site, tells this story...

I tell my girlfriends, "Get on this site, because I love you that much—get on this site! You're beautiful, men will love you." I have one friend—on a first date, she got $500 dollars—just for keeping the guy company. That's what some guys want— just company. In some ways, for guys who want company, it's kind of like being in a strip club. They feel they have an abundant amount of money— sometimes they just want someone to talk to— they'll pay more money for a girl who doesn't spread her legs than for girls that do.

Now look, I live in Atlanta and I date a lot of Caucasian men—I'm what you call overly attractive—a lot of white men love the way I look and want to be seen out in public with me—they just want to make other people jealous. This one guy, he paid me and a friend to come out with him to a strip club just to have the experience of walking through those doors with a woman on each arm. His amusement was to see us have a good time! He was a total gentleman. He didn't press for any sex or favors. He was nice—he had been really obese, but with lots of money. He told me he had got a gastric bypass—but I'm sorry, he was still unattractive physically. Worse, he still mentally sees himself as fat. But we had a good time, I was happy to help put a smile on his face. Why not?

Despite the popular mythology, men don't just want sex. They want companionship, conversation, someone to listen to them, to validate them.

Vivian, 40, has been married twice, raised children and traveled the world. Until she registered with WhatsYourPrice.com, she'd never been paid to go on a date, though it didn't seem that strange. "Men have given me money," she says, "but just because they wanted to. I consider myself priceless."

I have spent my life studying people and their behavior; I pay attention to eye contact, body language, etc., and I take a mental snapshot of the person. I ask questions with a reserved energy that pulls people in and gets them to open up quickly. People often tell me they feel as if they've known me all their lives. I offer compassion, a listening ear, and suggestions. When men want to have sex with me, I tell them to get in line. If that was what I wanted I'd consult my Rolodex. Wanting to have sex is a given, but engaging with me intellectually is more likely to get them there.

One of my dates bid $400. He was married to a disabled woman he loved and would never divorce, but he was looking for a sugar daddy arrangement on the side. Instead of giving me cash, he gave me jewelry. It was okay with me, but I only took one pair of earrings. We had a nice dinner and I could tell he was looking for intimacy—but I'm not interested in becoming a third wheel in someone else's relationship. I am a one-man woman—when I find that one man. The truth is I will have dinner with him again—no earrings—he's a good man who needs a friendly ear and some compassion. I feel like that's really what they're paying for on WYP— attention. Men will go to a strip club and pay someone to look into their eyes and listen to them. Why is that not okay, but it's all right to pay a psychologist $120 an hour? Why isn't it okay to pay someone for a date, or to have a relationship with them?

That need for companionship drives Michael, who works in a New Jersey warehouse—not high up in the office, but on the floor. Not wealthy at all, he joined WYP because he says it's his only chance to meet highly attractive women who will give him a few hours over dinner—even though it costs him a significant portion of his income. In fact, several men commented that they had spent their whole lives "settling" for dates or relationships with less attractive women and that WYP was their first opportunity to have the experience of being seated with a woman they consider truly beautiful. They are very open about the validation it makes them feel, or how they want to feel "used to" being with a beautiful woman, so that their skill levels rises and they won't feel so awkward when they meet hotter women in the real world.

And indeed, just as women are expecting a higher-quality man, someone with expendable cash who has made something of himself in the world, so too, men are expecting a higher-quality, more attractive woman.

Jack is a tough-talking businessman from a high-income neighborhood in Tennessee...

> On Match, they're just common old girls and common boloney. On WYP, I'm just saying there's a higher quality—more educated, prettier, more classy, they have more self-respect. They were exactly what I figured, and they were truthful about who they were, which was a nice surprise. In fact, I almost got too many at one time to handle them all....

One common theme I heard from women on the site is that they consider themselves "higher quality". They see themselves on WYP dwelling in the gray zone, somewhere between Match and a high-cost matchmaking service. They don't want to be out among the throngs on a Plenty of Fish, but neither do they have the inclination or resources to pay a high-priced matchmaker.

Bradley, a 41-year-old CEO of a small company in San Diego, is serious about getting married, finding the right woman. But he's among men all day, and wants to shortcut the process to finding classy women.

> *I like using the site. The women take it more seriously. They dress better, they write more intelligently, they put up good, quality photos. It's not a mass site. I show my buddies the photos—they like what they see. My friends get it—they understand I wouldn't do something like this just to mess around. I don't have time.*

I had a long, fascinating conversation with a WYP member named Rick. Appropriate to his training as a military officer and policeman, he walked me, with great observational detail through his experiences on other dating websites. His story encapsulates many of the truths we hear from other men on the site...

> *I'm a serious guy. I work hard. I'm fit, reliable, attractive. I have a child from another marriage. And I want to be married and live with the love of my life. I went to eHarmony because of their*

commercials but the only women they sent me were older and overweight and the ones I wrote to didn't respond. I actually called eHarmony's customer service and said, "Hey, why are you sending me older, overweight women?" They told me I needed to open up my mind! You know what I told them I needed to do? I need to end my subscription!

So he tried Match.com…

With Match.com, women kept writing but this weird thing kept happening. They said they wanted to get to know me better, they wanted to write back and forth, back and forth. I'm not a stalker, I'm not weird. I have a significant Internet presence, and I would tell them to Google me—I really put myself out there on Match and it was completely ineffective.

He tried Plenty of Fish and learned why it was so hard to get a date there…

On POF, any girl who's halfway attractive says it's overwhelming. My Xmas party date? She told me she had forty pages of e-mails the first day she was on POF. She told me she deleted her account because it was just too much to handle.

That explains something I noticed on sites like that. When I found pretty girls, it seemed they'd disappear the next day. Now I know why.

One night, he was watching *The Millionaire Matchmaker* on Bravo and thought he'd give that a try. "I tried Patti Stanger's site—they were all women from other countries and they were looking for me to send them money."

He considered, but didn't try Zoosk because "Zoosk is connected to my Facebook account and I didn't want my friends to know the details of my Internet dating."

He ended up on WYP and had his first date with an attractive woman within a week. Rick cautions men that, as on any site, you have to keep pressing the filtering process.

I'm in a major city, so I offer $100 right up front, which seems a fair price. A woman who asks you to spend $200 or above is not looking for long-term relationship, so that automatically disqualifies them in my mind.

Age is another filter for him. He states clearly in his profile that he is looking for a classy life-partner, that he's not a sugar daddy. Nevertheless, he still gets winks from younger girls in their twenties. "I have a cut-off at age 28. Anything younger than that, I don't think they are serious about finding a partner."

I call myself the Last Gentleman Standing because I am a genuine gentleman; something many women say they want, but few actually know how to handle. It's more than opening doors; it's respect, consideration and gentlemanly conduct. I'm no bad boy. I'm also no Sugar Daddy. And I'm very clear about that in my profile—if that is what you are looking for, I'm not your man. If you are looking for a companion—someone you can love and trust. I may be your Gentleman."

Money Talks; Bullshit Walks: Getting Real on WYP

"I've come to realize that men seem to put more value on and have more respect for the things they have to pay a lot of money for... Perhaps now they will put more value on the opportunity to get to know me."
—Lauren, 37

One quality about the site that many members on both sides of the aisle seem to appreciate is the clarity that money brings to the table. In a fluid, mobile world where talk is cheap and showiness can deceive, they find that money makes things real. And real fast.

As we've heard from women who complain about getting "letter bombed" on other sites, when men are paying a flat fee for an online dating service, or nothing on one of the big free sites, it costs nothing to send an e-mail. Or a thousand. As one sardonic female member of WYP puts it, men might send out letters "recreationally" on the other sites and then get scared if an attractive woman actually says yes. Money changes the equation. It shows her men are serious.

It's difficult for me to meet people here in Miami. It's all partying here. I work in the night, I'm a makeup artist and most of my clients are *weddings or I teach them after work—it's complicated to go out and I don't have many free nights. It's not a good idea to waste my time. I want to know a man really wants to meet me— and putting up $100 is a pretty good indication.*

—Sonia, 45

With the WYP system, men have to be *twice* as serious about the women they write to, because not only do they offer cold, hard cash for a dinner with a warm, soft woman, they also expend WYP credits every time a woman accepts a date. Eric, a financial industry type from Manhattan lays out the math on his end...

Guys can write to everyone on other sites. Here on WYP, I take it more seriously—I don't have unlimited credits—so I choose who I write to more carefully.

It also solves one of the biggest complaints both men and women have on other sites—the flaking-out factor. On the big sites, some people e-mail each other back and forth for fun or flattery or from boredom—and don't actually meet anyone in person. Many men express frustration with other sites because, without the money exchange, there is just no ballast to sustain momentum toward an actual date...

I really like to talk to girls on the phone first—once they agree on a price, I immediately move to exchanging numbers. One huge difference with other sites is that it's easier to advance to the phone. The money exchange makes it more serious, more like a business, it feels safer.

Indeed, when asked, men on WYP admitted that they got more dates, more efficiently. Brian works in the music industry in Los Angeles:

I have been on so many other sites...but THIS ONE WORKS! However, it has created a bit of a time-management problem for me. Other sites, my response rate was low, maybe 10 percent, 15 at most. Here it is closer to 60 or 70 percent. So I suddenly find myself totally overcommitted for dates with attractive, beautiful ladies... Oh well, there are worse problems to have, I suppose.

Several members of the site used the same phrase. They said, unlike other sites, WYP is "not about becoming pen pals." Rather, it's about shortcutting the online dating process and meeting in the flesh.

The gravity of the cash offer breaks the ice, demonstrates your seriousness about wanting that first date and, with rare exceptions, if it is accepted, gets you the first date right away. On other sites, so much more is left to chance. As members tell it, on other sites, it feels like letting loose hundreds of trial balloons. It may take an attractive women weeks to get around to your letter or your profile, because there is no hard, fast "offer on the table". The offer wakes up the attractive partner and gives her extra incentive to say "yes". As a result, dates can happen with lightning speed. Rick is a 42-year-old business owner...

I initially heard about it on ESPN radio—that pretty girls would go out with you if you pay them. I thought it sounded strange at first, but I looked at the site, saw the warning that first dates were not to expect sex and I slowly warmed to it. I went from the perception of I'm paying for sex to paying for the opportunity to have a pretty girl to go out with me. Plain and simple. It was December and I needed a date for a Christmas party, and let me tell you, I couldn't get a date to save my life on any other site. So I went on WYP and within a couple of hours—not days, hours—I had a date and we really hit it off. She was a real trouper, going to a party where she knew nobody, but everybody adored her at the party, me most of all. She was the belle of the ball. And four months later, we're still dating.

Doug is a straight-shooting New Yorker, early 50s, bearded, a millionaire several times over from businesses he's scratched together and sold off. If there was ever a dating site built for someone like Doug, this is it...

> *I kind of like that you don't have to put a bunch of bogus bullshit about walking on the beach or listening to love songs. Instead, you say what you want. You lay out what your requirements are for a date—body type, education, cultural and athletic tastes, and so forth. You say "I'm willing to spend 100 bucks to go on a date. And all I ask from you is that you tell the truth and show up like you agreed."*

Many women like the idea of money up front because it demonstrates a seriousness about the date that they don't find on other sites. Suzanne is a 57-year-old woman from Texas who found that dating again was not as easy as she thought. She seemed to be drawing the strangest men at all the extremes—and all of them unwanted.

> *I got married at 18, a good Texas girl. My husband had an affair so I have a real trust issue. So when I started on dating sites, the people I met weren't up-front about who they were, with their*

names, with what they do. Some of the guys were married... I seemed to attract them.

I tried Plenty of Fish—they have these mixers, to meet a whole bunch of singles. Everybody there was drinking heavily and were really, really old. I'm 56. I know I'm no spring chicken, but they were gray-haired and all bearded, 75 and 85.

On the popular dating sites, they just said, "Hey, meet at my place and have dinner." Meaning that they are cheap and don't want to buy dinner.

So I took my name off all the sites.

Then my girlfriend told me about WYP, my first thought was, oh, this could be fun! It's like going to benefits when people auction off dates, and it sounds like that!' And then I thought, if a guy has to pay for a date, he'd be more up-front about what he wants and what he wants in a relationship. That actually sounded refreshing, in a strange way. The fact that they are putting up money said to me that they're not just trying to invite you over for free.

On WYP, I accepted 5 offers—mostly around 80 dollars. The first one I accepted seemed to be pretty up-front. I accepted the offer but he never showed up at the date. Never called.

The second one—a guy from California, he offered to fly me out. I turned him down. He was thirty-something—as old as my son. I mean *seriously, what would a thirty-something guy be interested in a fifty-something-year-old woman.?*

The third date I accepted was local, so I accepted though his offer was only 30 dollars. He was self-centered, all about him, rude to waitstaff. Nothing was good enough for him. I learned I needed to screen more thoroughly. I'm not looking for hit-it-or-quit-it—I'm looking for a real relationship. If it develops into marriage, I would like to try that again.

The fourth date—he was respectful, walked me to my car like a gentleman and put the cash into it. I didn't ask. He said he was wondering if I would accept another date.

My fifth date? I'm dating him now. He offered 40 dollars, from a nearby town. He asked to meet for dinner. We clicked, he was cool. We've been to a movie, went shopping at Ikea, to the ice cream shoppe. He's been separated for five years and is almost divorced.

I like WYP better than the other sites. If they have to pay for dates, or if they volunteer to pay for dates, I figured they would have more of an interest in me, whereas on other sites, they're just looking for quantity over quality.

Lou, aged 71, who found his current girlfriend on WYP, concurs that the whole cash and credit-opening system prompts people into taking action.

> *If I have any criticism of WYP, it would be that I had to accept her offer and pay them before I could communicate with her. I understand that's how they make their money, and it's fair, I didn't even mind paying $20 for credits. I just didn't like that she had to accept the offer before I could even talk to her... but you know, maybe it's not so bad actually. Paying for a first date makes you a little more... I don't know...it kind of pushes you forward.*

Dating, flirtation, seduction—these are ancient games where truth is often a moving target. In fact, the whole process is often a dizzying, playful series of dips and dives, thrusts and feints, blustering, coyness, advances and retreats. A game of masks.

You could say the whole "game" aspect of flirtation and dating reached its mercenary apotheosis in Neil Strauss's book *The Game*, where every move, every garment, every word, every response is a calculated battle tactic. The goal is conquest of a "target", in the lingo of *The Game*—a phone number "close" or a kiss "close" or of course, a "closing of the deal".

It's an ironic use of language—or rather a sadly revealing one—because, to my mind, "opening" an authentic conversation is a completely different kind of game. Opening a relationship. Opening yourself up to learn, grow, connect. Opening a woman's heart. It's the opposite of the mercantile "closing" mentality of the pick-up artist.

As much as *The Game's* success as a best-seller shows that there is a public ravenousness for mastery of the strategic manipulation of a woman into a set of desired physical actions via the calculated deployment of fakery, so it seems that there is an equivalent desire to cut through the falseness, the masked thrust-and-parry gamesmanship of dating, and instead get to what's irrefutably real.

And as any business owner who negotiates a deal will attest, putting money on the table is the quickest way to "get real". You put up or shut up. Down clangs a barrier on falseness, coquettishness, big talk, and empty promises. There's a great Yiddish word for this moment: *tachlis*—a word related to buttocks and means literally, "the bottom line". When WYP allows men and women to put money into the equation, it's a way for each party to let down the guard and say, "I've got my cards on the table, and the money on the table requires that you do the same. Come on, let's figure out if we've got a real deal here. Date or no date?"

For many users of WYP, that straightforwardness is what draws them to the site and keeps them there—the desire to escape the batting-of-the-eyelashes, hide-behind-the-curtains, come-and-catch-me game of dating.

While for many, this kind of romantic foreplay delights, for other personality types, it's maddening. More than that, it's time-wasting and goes against their whole way of being and doing business in the world. This post appeared on WYP's open blog comments:

I decided I would give this a try as I like the concept because it's a put-your-money-where-your-mouth-is type of site AND women also have to be more sincere in accepting a date and not flake or be on here just to get their ego a boost. I am looking forward to trying this... I do not believe it's a pay for sex deal. It's kinda like when one wants to see a movie we must still purchase a ticket, right? Good luck to everyone on here!"

This commentator found that women on other sites may simply be enjoying the ego gratification of attention from men, and may end up standing him up. He is counting on the fact that the monetary transaction will work as more as a guarantee: that if she said she'd meet him she will actually show up. Glenn, a likable straight-shooter, a small blue-collar business owner in Phoenix, has found that to be true.

I see this as a great modern twist on dating— you're straight-up talking about topics that are going to come up during dating—but on WYP, everything's more planned out, everything's more on the table from the start. If you communicate, then you ARE gonna go out on a date, whereas on other sites, people drift in and out. There's more of a guarantee that you will go out. It's transactional—and in that way, it feels modern. Not like old-school dating, where everything is mysterious, you never know what's true, there are more games. This is easier, everything's clear and laid out—which is perfect for a busy guy like me.

Doug, the serial entrepreneur agrees:

I don't think its old-fashioned. I see it as contemporary—you're straight-up talking about topics that are going to come up anyway during dating—eventually—but on WYP, everything's more planned out, everything's more on the table from the start. If you communicate, then you are gonna go out on a date, whereas on other sites, people drift in and out. There's more of a guarantee that you will go out. It's transactional—and in that way, it feels modern. Not like old-school dating, where everything is mysterious, you never know what's true, there are more games. This is easier, everything's clear and laid out—which is perfect for a busy guy like me.

Similarly, the expectation created by a monetary exchange is that there will be more "truth in advertising". Says one New Yorker...

On other sites, women lie—that picture was five years ago—and it takes them half an hour to get out of the car—for each half! Hands down, there is more truth on this site—because it's a real deal. Men are paying and women are getting paid. And if that woman shows up on the date wobbling like a bowl of Jell-O, she won't get the money promised. And she shouldn't!"

Money, in every stratum and corner of society, gets people to sit up and pay attention. While some outsiders find the idea of spending money to buy a woman's time for a date to seem off-putting, even hideously objectifying, many of the actual members of WYP use the innocent analogy of "charity date auctions". In this charming parallel, they say that people "bid" for each other all the time for dates with hunky men or attractive women, all in good fun. A male member of WYP writes...

When I was 18, I was in a college charity auction where a girl bid for a date with me for five dollars. When we went out she treated me to pizza. The money part of What's Your Price can be fun if both people sincerely like each other, but it should be an extra incentive and not the main reason for going on the date.

Because the money at these "date auctions" goes to benefit charities and other worthy causes, most people consider them good, clean fun. At the same time, they carry an aura of naughtiness, of breaking a taboo— which adds a certain exciting edge. It wakes people up to possibilities outside normal, socially accepted pathways of connection. It opens up new possibilities for both parties. After all, you never know what will happen on that auctioned date. Exactly as true for WYP.

But whereas the fundraising kind of bidding is done in a spirit of play, most of the members on WYP are there for serious business. They really do want to find a romantic partner—and to do so efficiently. The more precise analogy for what is going on, really, is not the charity-auction comparison, but all the social/business ways that money often buys a place at the table.

In short—money opens doors.

For example, families buy more expensive houses to get their kids into the better school districts. Salespeople and executives join country clubs to pal around with potential clients. Brokers and agencies buy whole tables at charity dinners, not because they are passionate about particular charities, but because they are courting the important personages throwing the event, and look forward to hobnobbing with the other moneyed attendees. It's how things get done.

In nearly every area of life, when people are seeking to raise their position in the world and get what they want, they "buy a place at the table" to be among those they wish to be around. It's a normal and accepted business practice, both for men and for women. And in a society where money opens doors, it was really only a matter of time before someone popped up with the idea of buying a place at romance's table. Says Vanessa, an executive at a small company in Seattle:

> I am interested in meeting a man who has already built something in the world and not struggling. The man I want to meet is going to want to find me a catch. I'm smart, educated, and very attractive. I don't want to overstate it, but I bring a lot of value to the table. People pay for a lawyer's time, or a doctor's or a tennis coach or consultant in exchange for some kind of value. This is my value. It's maybe more obvious, and if a man is willing to pay for some time to see if we hit it off, I think that's a fair trade.

Is What's Your Price inherently fair or unfair? Many who castigate the site argue that by prioritizing look and money, it is cruelly unfair. Wade wouldn't disagree. "People usually meet over shallow things in the first place, anyway. But that doesn't mean something deeper can't spring from it. Look around. It often does."

There is no way to argue that What's Your Price—or any dating venue—is impeccably fair. But what's interesting and unique about this site is how one simple cash payment creates a special kind of fairness—or equalization—within the ecosystem of the site itself.

The Mysterious Alchemy of Cash: Money, Attraction, and Desire

The question that makes WYP a fascinating study of human behavior is "how does money function?" We have seen that it opens doors. That it makes people more "serious" and take the dating process more seriously. We have seen that it can be a knife that cuts through falsehood and gives an incentive to take a chance on somebody you might not otherwise consider as a romantic prospect.

On the other side of what we like, money also tends to give one a sense of deservingness, of privilege over others—but so does beauty. An *Evolutionary Psychology* report on a recent study of attractiveness had men and women rate themselves for attractiveness, look at a picture of a candidate for a hypothetical date, and then give their opinion of who should pay.

Across the board, good-looking women and handsome men were less likely to think they should have to contribute. As the researcher Michael Stirrat put it, attractive people feel they "quite literally bring more to the table, so they expect the other person to pick up the tab."

In the silent calculation of dating, then, the offering of money becomes an official statement of a greater desire. This plays out in many ways. For example, on a normal date, says Dr. Stirrat, "When a man offers to pay for the meal, he is to some extent saying, 'I'm interested, I'd like a second date, I'd like to see you again.'" Money, here, serves as a perceived equalizer, in case the woman at dinner has not clearly communicated her equal desire to have a second date. Again, we all like to think that looks and money shouldn't matter in the realm of the heart, but they do.

It is a common expectation that a less attractive man will often not hesitate to pay for dinner and all expenses. It brings the silent power balance even, as a new element of posited reciprocity is created. We may wish that men and women progress through the steps of intimacy side by side, but that doesn't always happen. Sometimes an extra prod is needed. Sometimes it's the paid-for dinner. Sometimes it's flowers, or a kind gesture. Sometimes it's a love letter. Sometimes it's sex. Both men and women wield whatever magical amulets they have to conjure the desired effect—and keep the journey moving forward.

According to psychological research, there is a natural equilibrium that allures couples. People generally choose mates with a similar level of attractiveness as themselves, the evolutionary theory being that by mating with someone whose genes are similar, the level of one's own genes are conserved or augmented. Money appears to provide an augmented sense of "survival" security, if not genetic, then practical. From the "attractive" side of the table, money is not merely a perk, but a perceived necessity. Rebecca, a WYP member, is a single mom:

> *How does money matter? It depends on what meaning people attach to it—for me, it's a way of leveling the playing field. You want to ask me out, you want me to feel comfortable and happy and replacing any lost wage is a big part of that. A man might approach it as paying for something, but from my side of table, you're affording me to be here. I want to, but I can't afford to. If I could afford to, if I didn't have a child, I'd go on dates all over the place—I love meeting people.*

Money not only functions to make a man attractive as a potential date in women's eyes, it also gives men courage to raise their bar when it comes to approaching more attractive women. Rebecca continues:

> *Every man I went out with, I wouldn't have gone out with otherwise. They were awkward at first. One man walked by me four times because he couldn't believe I was that attractive. Because—he told me later —he never in a million years would he have asked me out in person. "You're way too gorgeous." Turns out we're smitten and we're going out next week when he gets back from a*

trip. On the outside, he looks like an average 60-year-old sedentary writer—but he's witty, fast, funny, bent, and thinks faster than me. And it's so riveting and sexy to be with him. I could completely marry a man like that!

When money is offered and exchanged on *WYP*, the man is following an ancient pathway by proving he can provide for a woman; she's considering as an intimate partner a man who's shown he values her by offering resources. In theory, this signals that he is willing to take care of her (although there are never any guarantees, if there ever were, even back in caveman days). It's an exceedingly practical interchange. CEO Wade is practical if anything, a data cruncher. So he didn't come to the idea for this site based on what "should" work...

In a world where people are trying so hard to connect, I believe anything that helps them do so, including an exchange of money, is a valuable pursuit. We need to detach morality from dating methods, and focus instead on the pragmatic: what works.

WYP offers another, more cruel—yet "true"—kind of pragmatic function. Because there are dollars on the table, it establishes a more accurate sense of "value" on the open dating market. What are you really worth in the dating arena? Think you're a "catch"? Then why are you only getting $20 offers? On the other hand, do you think you're not that attractive? Then why are men offering you $150 regularly just to have the opportunity to sit down for a quiet dinner and see if the two of you have chemistry? Dollar amounts can clarify for a woman fairly quickly, how "attractive" they seem to a cross-section of men (although, admittedly, it is a cross-section of men who are willing to pay for the privilege of a date).

The introduction of money is a real eye-opener for men just as well. There are many men who don't believe they could ever get a date with a beautiful women because they underestimate the "quieter" qualities they have—their kindness maybe, their thoughtfulness. A man might discover he doesn't have to offer $200, but rather, his profile might be enough to win the date for as little as a $50 offer. And as sometimes is the case, she may be so smitten by who he actually is in person, that she returns the money at the end of the date. So the truth to which some men wake up while using this site is that they, in reality, didn't need the money at all to "equalize" their worth. But they *did* need it to make their worth visible in the arena of first impressions by getting the date in the first place.

Importantly, just as positive truths prompted by statements such as "you're so adorable, I had such a good time with you, I don't want the money," may arise from WYP, so too do negative ones. A guy can offer all the money in the world, but if his profile and attitude are odious, women will not take the date.

> *I turned down one guy in Florida—he said he had a yacht and wanted me to go sailing the Keys and Bahamas, but he wasn't nice about it, like he expected me to jump at the offer. But being in the middle of the ocean with a strange guy? I'd rather be on land than be shark bait. He raised his offer to $500 plus airfare—but he didn't get that the money was irrelevant. I wasn't biting.*

A guy like that can raise the offer all he wants, but he will soon wake up to the fact that no amount of money will raise his actual value high enough to get him a date with the kind of high-quality attractive woman he may desire. If he pays attention, he might learn something valuable.

Similarly, a woman who demands $300 for a date might find that very few men—and certainly the wrong kinds of men—are willing to go that high. She might have to adjust her self-overesteem.

In either case, money is a corrective to self-delusion. Says Wade, "More than anything, this is an interesting experiment for people to see what they are worth on the open dating market. How much would it take to get you to go out with somebody else? You're about to find out. You may not like the truth or you might love it!"

This kind of corrective information can be a very welcome thing. The truth is that, as individuals, we rarely have a firm grip on how we land in other peoples' perceptions. What's worse, our minds often function—despite our self-flattering notions—not as a rational judge of what is true and false, but rather as a cheerleader for what we *want* to believe.

In his eye-opening book *The Happiness Hypothesis*, Jonathan Haidt of the University of Virginia offers a humbling and searing metaphor for how our rational mind works. Traditional Western psychology has long described the mind as a triumvirate of ego, superego, and id, with the understanding that the id is a set of horses, reined in and guided by the aware driver of the calculating ego, with the superego riding in the coach nagging the driver about how he's driving and letting him know where he *should* go.

Not accurate, says Haidt. Rather, the id is more than a powerful, lustful team of horses. It is a wild elephant trampling through the forest, and the driver (the ego and superego) is but a stick-thin little guy clutching to the sparse hairs high on the elephant's back—hanging on for dear life. In this picture, the ego, or rational mind, is not guiding the elephant of desire at all, but rather conveniently conjures up rationalizations to justify the elephant's destructive path.

You can see this in the way that well-meaning girlfriends bolster each other by telling each other how beautiful they are. In truth, they probably see each other's *inner* beauty more clearly than men would, who are driven more at first by outer beauty. But it can be a damaging inflation of self-estimation. Women, as Lori Gottlieb points out in her book *Marry Him: The Case For Mr. Good Enough*, women thus begin to mistake "desire" for "deserve". Reflected in the inflated flattery of each other's comments, they come to believe they all deserve someone like the character "Big" from *Sex and the City*.

Over in the men's room, you also see the impact of this inflation in the way that men suck their guts in front of gym mirrors, imagining themselves Adonises, and locking THAT picture into their minds as their self-image for the evening. As if women won't see the muffin-top wobbling over their ornamented belts. It's an old truth that men see a far handsomer self in the mirror, and women just the opposite.

WYP can also wake up women to just how attractive they are to men, where they might not have suspected it before. Deluged by images of dazzling gods and goddesses in popular magazines and media, both men and women begin to downplay their value on "the open market". Women begin to think they can't compete with flashy blondes wielding silicone Hindenbergs—but they forget that there are whole classes of men who see those super-Barbies as screaming warning signals of "Danger!" Many men find that kind of superficiality comical, or deeply ugly on multiple levels. These men value what other, less ornamented women have to offer, whether it be their warm hearts, their solid, reliable values, their athleticism, sense of adventure, intellect, humor, talent or any one of a hundred other estimable qualities. And when you look at the female profiles on WYP, you see all those qualities expressed robustly.

So, too, men often think they need the speedy car or scintillating quip to capture the heart—and other anatomical parts—of a beautiful woman, though again, this is patently not true. Passion, purpose, loyalty, strength of character, artistry, humor, playfulness, intelligence—these are often the qualities that ignite a woman's attraction and devotion.

In all these ways, WYP is in the tradition of the site www.HotorNot.com, which functions the same way—it gives you a dispassionate crowd-sourced judgment strictly on your looks and first impression. You post a photo and the anonymous Internet masses grade your attractive on a scale of 1–10. A few hundred, a few thousand votes, and you get a pretty reliable estimation of your generally perceived hotness. Or not-ness.

Similarly, with WYP, though not as statistically significant, a man or a woman can get a fairly reliable read on his or her "first impression" desirability, based on where the dollar amount starts and stops. To some, it may hurt their feelings. To others, it may stoke their ego. But in either case, a kind of truth is revealed.

Finally, there is what appears to be the "darker" side of money. In these cases, it creates a service-based relationship that is not heart-based in any traditional meaning of that word. This is where we hit the world of "sugar daddies" and "sugar babies".

Wade explicitly states on the site that it is not meant to be used for escort services or prostitution and, as he has publicly stated repeatedly, he boots escorts off the site right away. However, there are plenty of women who, while not being "escorts" in any professional way, are clearly on the site looking for men who can provide them not with merely cash for a date, but cash on an ongoing basis. Men are generally hip to who is whom. Grant is from San Diego...

> *I watch out for gold-diggers—I'm on alert for coded messages like "I'll be more than generous in return for a generous guy" or "let's have dinner—and then we'll decide if you want dessert". I don't judge them for that—they're being straight-up and some guys are looking for that. It's honest. We're adults. Honesty is good. It's just not what I'm here for.*

Obviously Brandon and his team, while reviewing every profile individually to assure that escorts are not trolling his site, cannot control what happens on a date or afterward. Men can try to flip the first date into an ongoing compensated relationship, and women can make offers to men for the same.

Women on the site are curiously tolerant of the idea of Sugar relationships, even if that is not what they are looking for, themselves. Maria, who lives in Houston, says:

> *It's not for me but I understand it. I have friends. I've seen it work. A sugar relationship can be loving and conscientious. I think it's fine if sugar daddies want to pursue women who aren't trying to get married and have babies. They both can get a lot out of it. What's really sad is the opposite—when a man who doesn't want babies getting a young woman bonded and wasting her baby bearing years.*

Rebecca, the scientist-nerd-hottie agrees that just because money is involved in an ongoing relationship, doesn't mean that it can't be a mutually enriching experience.

> *I met a guy on WYP who I truly came to love. He knew that we couldn't have a real relationship— he traveled too much but we wanted to be generous with each other—how could I not be a*

nag and compete with his work and how could he support my education—it was so clean, so full of integrity—he offered a stipend and we would make love from time to time—it was as intricate and custom-made as any individual human being. There was true compatibility and trust.

While WYP isn't built for this kind of Sugar relationship, she insists that it's a perfectly viable alternative relationship for two adults.

Stop prejudging sugar relationships as an obstacle—it only makes you dumber and dumber. People have an opinion before knowing anything about it—not to mention they're missing out on unbelievable opportunities to make enriching, meaningful connections with intelligent, kind, generous, sensual, vital, human beings who want to connect with someone else.

Sugar relationships turn out to be far more complex than the popular conception, certainly more so than this author imagined when he began interviewing people on this site. They clearly answer very specific emotional needs for men, as well as both financial and emotional needs for women. Sex, curiously, is not always at the center—or involved at all.

Many sugar relationships have no sexual exchange at all. Many sugar daddies are married men who just want to be treated well by a young woman. They want the kindness, they want the admiration, they want the youthful optimism of a young woman in their lives. Sometimes they'll put young women through college, just to have the experience of gratitude and of helping out, but don't want to cheat on their wives, so sex is off the table.

Many Sugar relationships are driven by career needs. On the male side, many successful men have little or no time to date or look for a complex relationship. In fact, they studiously want to avoid one that would be dramatic, time-consuming, complicated, and inconvenient. And those men are perfectly willing to bring their resources to guarantee a regular female companion for outings, for sex, for company, for travel. Only sometimes do these have the john/hooker dynamic, as these women are often adventurous and educated, and the relationship can be based on genuine friendship and mutual respect.

On the women's side, there are many who prefer a Sugar situation because they don't want the time and bother of a complicated, dramatic relationship, either. Their priority is not on "giving myself to a man" but rather to develop their lives and careers, or focus on raising their kids. Says one woman, "I want to have an intimate partner, but I don't have the time for a full-on relationship with all that entails." Some women explicitly want exposure to professional men who know something about the world, who can introduce them to "the right people", who can get them out of their small towns, their limited circles, and offer them new experiences in the world. Many sugar daddies are happy to help enterprising sugar babies get started in their own businesses. In the end, Sugar relationships bring together people with complementary needs. Emily lives in Chicago, and has been on WYP for four months:

There's one man courting me now, he had an eight month relationship with a woman finishing her masters degree—she wanted the opportunity to make love, but she had little time. She was putting herself through school. His assistance allowed her to quit her job and focus on her studies. When she graduated, she moved to Chicago—and started her life on her own, and they are friends to this day...

Big Fish, Hope, and Aphrodisiacs: The Emotional Gravity of Money

Last year, I was flying across the country and fell into conversation with the attractive nurse in the seat next to me. When we turned to our professions and I said that I am a high-end dating coach and expert, her eyes ignited with delight. "Oh my god," she exclaimed, as women often do, fascinated that someone could actually figure this stuff out. "I have so many questions!"

"Let's start with one," I suggested. "The hardest one."

"Okay," she pondered. Okay..." She thought and thought. Then said, "Okay, so what's up with all the fish!?"

"Fish?" I asked her? And she proceeded to school me on the mating habits of Minnesotans. Apparently men's dating profiles there are replete with photos of dudes holding up freshly caught trout, walleyes, and perch.

I told her the reason men were holding up fish was an ancient one. It is the same reason men in L.A. take photos of themselves in front of their Maseratis. Why men in Boston snap themselves on the bows of their 34-foot sailboats, and why Montanans pose in front of shot elk. Women, after hundreds of thousands of years of evolutionary training, seek men who can provide *resources*. And men, somewhere in our murky brains, know this, and create rituals of resource display in the early stages of dating.

This is a universal pull, that, at its base, attraction is rooted in a man's ability to procure resources. And money is the most obvious form of resources in the modern world, the most fluid, the most outwardly powerful and the most flexible. Money makes things happen, above and beyond forestalling starvation. (Although I teach men in my programs that, in reality, a man's reputation, his network of friends, his adaptability, the closeness of his family, his sense of humor, his education and his stick-to-it-iveness are also all highly valued resources, and should be displayed for similar effect, and for similar reasons.)

Money, despite its established, familiar place in the romance and marriage game and its practical utility, nevertheless remains an emotional hot-button issue. And it will stay that way simply because some people have it and other people don't. It creates an immediate inequality between people, and something inside us intuits that we should all be deemed equal in the eyes of God, the law, and each other. We are all human beings who bleed, love, suffer, dream, die—and there is, at root, a natural equality of soul, if you will.

But if we are equal as human beings, how then should resources be divided? Marx famously proscribed, "From each according to his ability; to each according to his need." But that has a funny way of demotivating those with ability. To others, pure merit should determine who has more money. If someone has skills, hard-work, innovation and persistence, well then, surely that person "deserves" more money. To these people, those who have gamed the system, such as inheritors and financial swindlers, have an unjust claim on their riches.

To still others, money should go in proportion to how much good a person supplies to society, to the commons. The fact that a shill for big pharma, dancing her way through doctors' offices offloading the latest deadly (but only via side-effects) pill gets compensated at 4x or more a hardworking schoolteacher seems not only offensive but downright destructive to the good of all.

And finally, there are the Hobbesian free-marketers, who say, strip back government and let loose the dogs of economic war—and may the most clever/brutal/dominant win.

Each of these beliefs carries benefits—and each carries costs.

The thing is that money, by its nature, puts a universal value on qualities that are not universally admired. So it is inevitable that someone will always be pissed off by some perceived inequality. Someone will always find the current distribution of money unjust.

Similarly, somebody will always find offensive the universal "objectification" that money as the universal currency puts on seemingly all aspects on our lives. For example, how do you put a price on love? On friendship? On acceptance? You can't, of course, and shouldn't.

That is why emotions are especially raw around the realm of love. There is a subtle (and sometimes not so subtle) weight put on various "resources" that men and women bring to the dating market. Beauty and health and youth are resources. So is money. So when money is put on the table—if only to open the door to love, as is the mission of WYP—red flags shoot up all over the place.

"This objectifies women!"

"This demeans women—is that all we are worth? Fifty bucks?"

Yes, it's true, at first blush, something sounds awful about the whole process. It feels spiritually base. And yes, through one lens, at first sight, bidding a hundred dollars for a date may sound like the ultimate objectification of a woman and the ultimate exclusion of good but poor men. It growls with privilege. It rings with distant echoes of slave auctions, the idea that you can "have" a person for a set amount of money. But it doesn't take much digging to make the clear distinctions. The generous man doesn't get to drag the woman home in chains and demand her service. He can't "have" her at all. She is perfectly free to say no. And if she does say yes, he is merely "renting" her time for a few hours, just as he might a consultant, a lawyer, a psychologist, or a massage therapist. A lawyer will give you an hour's worth of legal advice. A bodyworker, a nice, vigorous massage. And on a WYP date, the "utility" you are purchasing is the time of an attractive woman in order for you to make the case that you are a man worthy of her attention.

That is the exchange. If there is no chemistry, hands are shaken, cheeks may be kissed. In the best of all possible worlds, good luck may be sincerely wished, and as after most dates elsewhere, separate ways are taken. The deal is done.

If, however, chemistry is sparked, the second date and anything beyond occurs on the same level playing field as any other dating process. The emotional gravity of money fades. As Brandon Wade says:

> *Money doesn't place value on a "woman"—on her "soul" or anything like that. It places a monetary value on the opportunity to win the heart of a certain woman. As a man, or as the generous partner, you are valuing her time. That's all. Now it's up to you to bring to bear your charm, your intelligence, your kindness, and whatever tricks you have up your sleeve to win her interest.*

So even if it's far from "prostitution", WYP can still feel like objectification because you're hanging a price tag. But broadly, this is the common cultural way of showing that you value something. In fact, it's the *most* common way in our culture of showing that you value something. When a man blows a month's salary on an engagement or wedding ring, isn't he doing something similar? Money, for better or worse, is how men, in particular, demonstrate how they put value on what they care about. Some women rail at this; some have called it "demeaning", "abuse", and in the explosively exaggerated words of Dr. Callahan on the Anderson Cooper Show, "traumatic".

This initial moment of valuation is often unsaid in the dating world, but it is no less real. Men will confess that the more beautiful or desired a woman, the better the restaurant to which he will take her. Correspondingly, the more acute a woman, the more precisely she can read a man's unsaid "valuation" of her at the start based on what's on the menu!

Wade points out that in our culture, almost everywhere, men and women come together over superficial things, and it's usually looks, muscles, or money. And it is this hot-or-not calibration that keeps some women off the site. Some people don't want to know their "number", and want to persist in the hope that they will be evaluated by the opposite sex for their inner worth. What if you are valued lower than your self-image? When he was doing an interview on Playboy Radio, the bunnies on air with him fretted, "What if I don't get offers? Or what if a guy offered me five bucks? Does that mean I'm worth five bucks? I would feel so insulted!"

By now it should be obvious that the offered money doesn't represent a perception of an attractive woman's "worth"—it only represents specific men's valuation of her time, based on a whole stew of considerations, foregrounding physical beauty along with what she says in a few lines on a profile. It doesn't measure her soul. If one man offered her five bucks, that would be a reflection of his particular combination of tastes, resources, and attitudes. If twenty guys in a row offered five bucks, well then, she might want to pay attention to that and lead with other virtues.

Naturally, the same is true for the woman who registers, worried she'll be offered $50 and finds that she receives consistent offers for $100 or above. This woman will quickly learn that she has been underestimating her "value" on the open market. Says one happily surprised member...

> *I never had to ask for the agreed-upon amount—I always get more. I ask and they agree. They usually give the amount when they pay the check, or in the beginning of the dinner along with typical questions—"What's your experience on this site—oh, here, I have to give you the money." I've never had trouble with anyone. They are very*

gracious with me, but remember, I do filter a lot before I go out with anyone. Out of maybe twenty offers, I go out with three.

Money can serve not only as a pleasant surprise or nasty shocker, it can also work as an aphrodisiac. Says Albert, the PhD from the Bay Area:

I've asked women why they are on this site—[they say] "I'm tired of dating guys on Match.com that can't even afford to take me to lunch." I like that I am comfortable, and I like to show a woman a good time. That makes a man attractive—this goes to the primordial draw—women want to be provided for. Sure there are women who just want to go on a meal and get 150 dollars and have no intention of going a second time. But I'm looking for a relationship leading to marriage...

In a recent BBC series on love, the producers showed women random photos of male potential dates—along with each one's salary printed below. They raised and lowered the salary on different cards and then asked the women to rate the men solely on their looks. Across the board, higher salaries translated to higher "attractiveness" ratings. The pictures, of course, didn't change. Perception did.

Possessing money conveys not only safety now, but a promise of future action. On a primal level of masculine/feminine attraction, it often represents the ability of a man to make his will felt in the world. Unless he was born into it, surplus money indicates that he is smart, persistent, and has the power, in whatever form, to shape the will and behavior of people around him. It broadcasts that he can get things done. It is a form of power, and that, simply, is sexy. Conversely, lack of money often suggests a man's lack of ability to make his will felt...

I could overlook his looks, belly, or even that unsightly strand of nose hair for practical reasons, because I know what's more important. On a side note, I have a set of ideals and expectations of a man. I will not date a poor chap because more often than not he is either lazy, not very bright, or not hard-working.
—Gina, 29, Los Angeles

A man who is effectual is, on a primal level, a man to whom a woman feels she can entrust her future. In reality, riches might prove nothing but that he is a cheat, a manipulator, or a con man—but that's the exception. The perception of women is clearly that the men here are of a higher quality.

And most men have found that WYP attracts a "higher-quality" woman. It is a judgment that is not limited to looks. Jack is a martial-arts instructor from the Midwest and a successful businessman...

Sure, I think a bunch of the women on the site just want money. But on the whole, the women on this site are better-looking, more sophisticated. They figure if a guy is willing to pay, they know I'm not some broke guy. The ladies are looking for some kind of security. If you're willing to give 'em 200 bucks for a date, you get totally a different genre of women—a higher quality, a more serious type of woman who knows more. Who expects more out of life and puts in more effort. Some are more old-fashioned, some are more modernized, up-to-date ladies, you have all kinds.

The fact is, our caveman history still powerfully affects our mating behavior. Carol Cassell, president of the Society for the Scientific Study of Sexuality, spent three years researching human sex appeal, and found that financial security across all cultures is so important to women that they will forego good looks in a mate, or a sense of humor, or even intelligence, as long as the man offers security and protection for her and her offspring.

Cassell also found that women's inability or refusal to separate love from sex isn't merely a myth, nor a mere by-product of socialization; rather, it too is connected to women's role as child-bearers and nurturers. In the cave, it was relatively simple. Women sought out those males likely to deliver the most protein (meat, Minnesotan fish) to build strong children, and to keep her safe to perform her mothering tasks. Today it's more complex: she's looking for a guy who'll pay tuition for the best schools, orthodontia, music and dance lessons, baseball uniforms, fancy summer camps—plus spa treatments or whatever it takes to keep *her* going, as well.

Taking the emotional trigger of money one step deeper, we discover that money not only functions as an attractor, it also functions as an aphrodisiac. In a recent study of the habits of more than 600 high-net-worth people, Hannah Shaw Grove and Russ Alan Prince, found a majority said that having money enhanced not merely safety, but their *sexual experiences.*

Some 84% of rich women and 63% of rich men said having money led to better sex—many even cited it as the main benefit of being rich. While men placed more value on quantity (number of encounters), nearly 93% of the women named higher-quality sex as the biggest benefit. The researchers attribute this to the sense of empowerment that comes with financial independence.

As writer Joan Didion once put it, "The secret point of money and power in America is neither the things that money can buy nor power for power's sake...but absolute personal freedom, mobility, privacy." It seems that the more you feel better about yourself, the more you can relax and enjoy giving and receiving physical intimacy.

WYP introduces another kind of empowerment. When a man bids a high amount to date a woman, it's proof of her desirability, and, as many women have admitted, the offer often makes her feel more empowered. Therapist Felice Dunas agrees that money can represent sexual power. On her website, she writes:

Power is a great aphrodisiac and money is all-powerful, so they go together like the cream and the cookie in an Oreo. Cultures throughout history have hooked them up, from dating to dowries to divorce settlements. Even in ancient times, men with greater resources married younger women, married more women, and produced offspring earlier, while those who did not have substantial resources or status were less capable of establishing long-term relationships. Across a wide variety of societies, male reproductive success is a function of social and economic status."

As one woman in a WYP discussion noted, "A man that is not generous with his money will not be generous with his affections. Every woman knows that." Whether true or not, that is a common perception. Dunas concurs with the idea that money has erotic promise, pointing out that even married couples who've been in a relationship for a long time can benefit by spending money...

> Want great sex tonight? Spend money today! If you think it is unwise to use one to attract the other, you are wrong. It works! A little gift at just the right moment will allow her to open herself to you with excitement rather than fear. Is this being manipulative? Not if you're sincere... Spend the dollars, relish your lust, feel the yearning, and enjoy the passion. Use all the tools you have at your disposal; free yourself from a life of quiet desperation.

It is important for daters to know that as significant as the *amount* that is spent, is *how*. For example, nothing kills the eroticism of a first date than a man pulling out a coupon for dinner when the check comes. And there is implied abundance in the man who tells the bellboy, the doorman, and the driver, "Keep the change."

"I was at the spa one day," commented a woman on

the WYP discussion group, "when a guy from this site who I hadn't yet met asked via text what I was doing. When I told him, he went to the spa's website and paid $500.00 for my day. I am certainly looking forward to meeting him now!"

Alicia, a 32-year-old who lives in the Philadelphia area, is straight-up about her intentions...

I've been online dating. I got tired of general dating websites because so many guys wrote me who were not living up to their potential. I work hard but I'm looking for a guy to take care of me. I need a guy to be financially able to take care of me. I was fed up. I want a man to say "save yours, here's mine."

Of course, there is a dark side of money's power, where men (usually) feel privileged to take what they want. Jenee, a religious-leaning sultry beauty of 32, tells a story that suggests that the flavor of her sexuality brings out exactly that quality in men, and not all of them wealthy. Sadly, she seems to have decided that it destines her to a life of lovelessness.

I'm the Angelina Jolie vibe, not Jennifer Aniston. Guys pick up on my sexual energy—they don't see me as wife material. It's my energy, too. I'm playful, fun. They don't treat me like wife material. When I meet a conservative guy—they think I'm too much for them—too much energy—too wild for him. But that's the kind of man I want.

I went on Match, which turned out to be full of liars; they claimed they were Christian, but I soon found out they were not. I went on Millionaire Match and got really spoiled by multimillionaires that I met. They took me to fancy shows. I've never been treated that way before, but I was just 1 out of 100 that they were playing. They treated me well but didn't take me seriously.

So I tried eHarmony—but I was not matched with anyone right and I hated the screening process. Plenty of Fish didn't pan out. I tried Christian Mingle—thinking it was more toward my values. I flew to Florida to meet a man I met there— he jumped on me, practically raped me.

I came on to What's Your Price because I was so tired of men using me as this girl they just want to sleep with all the time. I was tired of giving my heart. I drive to those dates, I get all pretty—but I don't get a relationship.

I came here out of bitterness. I should get paid for the fact no one wants to stay with me. I joined about six or seven months ago. It's paying off for me, so far. Guys on the site—some are vulgar, some are kind of "give me something". They are trying to get what they can on the first date. But I don't feel *bitter. I've met producers and multi-millionaires. They are like, I don't have a lot of time, but they will treat you to really nice places, spend a lot of money, they're busy. I ask my dates why they have chosen WYP, why would they pay for a date? Guys say girls are prettier on this site. They say it's the caliber of looks—they can't access this kind of woman in their everyday life."*

I would suggest that Jenee is fishing in the wrong ponds, or at least with the wrong bait. If she has not yet wholly given up on the possibility of love, she might be well-advised to turn down her self-presentation, and focus on attracting a man of character, first and foremost. Awash in wave after wave of money's lustful hunger, she has drifted far from the shores where hearts, unadorned, can meet. True romance becomes a distant mirage.

Culturally, we find the idea of a wealthy man paying for or "claiming" attractive women to be archaic, not politically correct, and also bereft of romance. You can't "buy" destiny, can you? Hollywood, in fact, prioritizes the very opposite quality of *randomness* as romance's spark in the classic "meet cute" moment—that adorable instant when his and her dogs' leashes get intertwined, when Sally and Harry end up having to drive across the country together, when Meg Ryan hears the lovelorn Tom Hanks on a late-night radio talk show.

Randomness creates a feeling of fate intervening, that it was "just meant to be". It's delightful. Certainly more delightful than a C-note plunked down on the table at Ruth's Chris.

However, as delightful as a "meet cute" can be, it's really just a convenient technique screenwriters use to bump two people together and get the action rolling. Dramatically speaking, it's an artificial ice-breaker that allows two people to start a conversation. Brandon's idea was that a simple monetary exchange could allow two people to get the ball rolling—equally. And, just as the movie couple's development will not be defined by the intertwining leashes, once they are initially untangled, so too the money issue drops away after the first date and the artificial launching mechanism of cash exchange becomes irrelevant.

And indeed, many members confess that if the date goes well, they often forget about the cash. Sometimes the money is returned (in one case I know of, a prominent attorney met a woman on this site who bought him a GoPro camera for his upcoming ski-trip before their fourth date). Sometimes the woman pays for the second date. And once a couple launches into these additional outings, the cash exchange becomes just a memory.

And, as it happens, just as Wade envisioned it, sometimes, a deep, lasting love blooms—even in the most unexpected places, or in this case, decades. Lou is 71 and he met his girlfriend, 50, on WYP in October, 2011. Befitting his cautious, fact-checking approach to life, they spoke on the phone every day for almost two weeks. Finally they met for lunch, and they liked each other so much they went out that same night. They've been seeing one another ever since.

My first thought [of WYP] was that it was an escort site. I saw women who seemed to be professionals. You can always tell—their photos are kind of glamorous. I didn't bother with those. The only women who responded, before M., were college girls looking for someone to help them through school. I saw very few profiles of women over 50. My daughter, who is 45, thought the whole thing was funny and warned me I'd better not to go out with anyone younger than her.

I wanted someone who lived nearby. I guess I didn't have great expectations, so I was surprised by M., not so much that we met, but that we hit it off so well. She asked $100 for a first date, and I thought "What the heck, it's not hard to spend $100 for a date," plus, she was within driving distance.

M. really wanted to meet someone to seriously date. She was at a crossroads in her life, and had only recently felt ready to begin going out again after her kidney transplant and five years of dialysis. She was a great gal. She had gotten engaged to a fella after her operation, but her fiancée unexpectedly died. It wasn't an easy time for her. Because of her condition, she was unable to work and couldn't get a job. But she's a fighter. We've been together ever since. I help her out a little bit with her expenses, but I'm retired and in no position to play Sugar Daddy.

You know, a strange thing happened recently. One Sunday I took her out to breakfast and told her I thought she might be better off finding someone who has more money to spend on her, someone closer to her age. I was just trying to help, to be pragmatic, but she started crying, thinking I wanted to break up. That whole episode made us even closer.

While there is a whole stew of emotional triggers caused by the cash element of WYP, ultimately, its importance fades away before more powerful forces of chemistry, lack of chemistry, or in the case of Lou and M., of love. But in those first few moments, the initial cash payment may cause both men and women to be faced with some turbulent soul-searching regarding their initial perceived "value" on the open market. It may add a stimulating spice of naughtiness, of breaking taboo. It bolsters many men, giving them the feeling of being more "manly" and in control of their destiny because their money helps them solve the problem of finding attractive women in the midst of busy schedules. And many a woman has confessed to the good feeling that, unlike elsewhere, here she's dating a man who's shown that he values her and is willing to put his money where his mouth is. In the end, the emotions WYP's unique meet-up system evokes are as varied as the flavors of *eros* itself. As Wade says:

Each of these elements can heighten excitement, can increase anticipation and add a new spice to dating. At the very least it's a lively, interesting way to date. And if we're bringing people together in a fun, efficient, safe way, there's no harm. Chemistry can spark anywhere. Why not here?

Part III:
WYP: A User's Primer

"Success depends upon previous preparation, and without such preparation there is sure to be failure."
—Confucius

Step 1: The Profile

Because I am a writer and high-end coach in the worlds of dating, attraction, and intimacy, both men and women often ask me for "rules". Some of the most common questions include...

- What should I say on my profile?
- Which pictures should I put in my profile?
- How forward should I be?
- Should I call first?
- How many days should I allow before calling her again?
- Which is the proper date for sex?
- How do I know if a woman wants me to kiss her or not?
- How do I let a man know I like him without seeming like a slut?
- How do I keep my sexual energy alive out in the world during the day so I can attract the right man when he comes along—without attracting the wrong men?
- What works always?
- What works never?

There are, of course, no formulas that work every time. What's Your Price uniquely transforms some of the vagueness of dating and makes some things—like honesty and clarity—work especially in your favor. It also raises new questions. For example:

- What's the optimal amount of money to offer?
- Should I counter-bid?
- How and when do we actually handle the financial transaction?
- What's the story with the second date?
- What expectations are there once money has passed hands?

I can tell you that if there is one monumental truth that will utterly determine your success in finding what you want on WYP, it's to be *searingly clear* about what you are seeking and what you will tolerate. Remember, because this is such an innovative and new site, the people at the other end of the fiber-optic are often as confused as you are!

In surveying a swath of members on their experiences on the site, the biggest complaint by far was disappointment that the date had been not clear about what they truly wanted. Men were distressed to discover women who said they were looking for relationships were really looking for sugar baby opportunities or just a free dinner and some cash. Women were distressed that men who acted respectfully in their profiles and in conversations would make aggressive offers of more money for sex at the end of dinner.

While these occurrences aren't prevalent, they tend to make both men and women sour to the dating experience. The solution: be clear what you want— whether it's a long-term relationship or short-term, no-strings-attached fun. Don't lie and don't mislead. It's not fair to the majority on the site who are straight-shooters.

Lies are rife on all online dating sites (actually, off them, too!) but you can arrange your experience so that you avoid them as much as possible. According to a study conducted at Cornell University, 80% of people on all dating sites lie about something in their profiles. The majority of these lies aren't very significant, and they're about what you'd expect from males and females respectively: men overstate their height by a mere 2%, while women reduce their weight by a slim 5%. The lies only get big enough to lengthen a nose when the situation is more extreme, such as if a man with dwarfism tacks on an ambitious six inches, or an obese woman magically sheds 50 pounds.

So consider this final section of the book a kind of bonus, a guidebook for your success—as well as a stand for rigorous truth. It turns out that truth will set you free—*free to get the experience you actually want.* Drawing on years of coaching, study, workshops, writing, and publishing on the dance of dating, I am going to give you best practices on constructing a profile, then on navigating the offer phase, the conversation phase, and finally the date. By the time you read this final section of the book, you will be far better prepared to succeed on WYP. In fact, as some of these truths go rather deep, you will be far better prepared to succeed in your dating and intimacy life across the board.

Note For Both Men and Women

As with all online sites, stay alert for scammers, con artists and grifters. They're female as often as male, and can be found on ALL Internet dating sites. While I am not a fan of ethnic stereotyping, the fact is that many do come from Eastern Europe. One man who's been dating online for four years, including on WYP, told me he was fooled once only, and lost $300 on the scam. "These Russian women are on every website across the Internet," he said. "They ask for plane fare (to come see you of course), or for money to bribe an official so they can to get out of the country (again, just to see you). They invent elaborate stories about violent husbands trying to murder them, or an official who wants to send them to a gulag."

If you inadvertently date a scammer, be sure not to give him or her money, or any financial information such as your bank account number. Once you realize you're dealing with a scammer, run as fast as you can in the opposite direction! And cut off all interaction.

If you want to fly someone out to meet you, send a plane ticket, not cash. And never, ever, ever send cash to someone you haven't met. Scammers come up with all kinds of elaborate stories to get you to send money. The rule about sending money is simple.

Don't. Ever.

Tips for Men

As with all dating profiles, be specific, be direct, tell the truth, stand for something big or lofty, be a bit sensual to show that you are sensually awake, add a dash of fantasy/romance, and hope and most of all, be straightforward about what you want.

Again, WYP is an unusual site because you can—and are expected to—be up-front about what you're looking for. For example, if you are seeking a life partner or long-term relationship, say it clearly and, better yet, say *why*.

To wake up her senses, paint a picture of what it will feel like for her to be with you. This is way of subtly inflaming her erotic imagination and also communicating you at your romantic best. Include a line of something like…

> *If the chemistry is good and we really click, we can look forward to lots of laughter, lots of weekend trips up along the coast, where I want to show you my favorite little nooks and wineries…*

When adding a simple line like this where you envision the future together, use the word "we" and include gatherings with friends if that's part of your picture (it invokes trust), cuddling and whatever activities you truly love—boating, hiking, theater—whatever is true for you. Men make the mistake in their profiles of just listing their assets as they perceive them, their accomplishments and position in the world. It often comes off as cold and dorky. I call this the "garage sale" profile, where men just matter-of-fact lay out all their perceived assets on the profile, the way you'd spread out your old lamps and picture frames on a driveway to make a few bucks before you move. Instead, add life by projecting only a dash of an alluring fantasy future to ignite her imagination.

If you are seeking a Sugar relationship, then be very clear about that in your profile. Don't be coy with statements like "and you know what that means". State exactly what you envision, what kind of dates, what kind of trips, the fact that you don't mind helping a great gal out with her bills or however you want to frame the relationship. The more clear you are, the less you involve women who are on the site for a more traditional relationship and the more appropriate your match will be when she reads you profile.

Here are some other ideas to make your profile stand out, drawn from my comprehensive guidebook to irresistible profiles, www.DeepOnlineAttraction.com.

Photos

I often talk about the impact of "Electric Contrast"—put up, at most, four photos that show different sides of you—so women don't pigeonhole you, or reduce you to a narrow idea before you even meet. Include one photo of you looking sharp and professional in a suit or tux, one athletic and brawny, one social and relaxing with friends (which shows you are not a lone wolf or cabin-dwelling ax-murderer) and one unusual snapshot to stand out and make them take notice.

For this final photo, do something outrageous and different. For years, I used a photo of me petting a wild tapir in the Amazon jungle—it's a pig-like creature that is actually related to the elephant. Women would write, "What is that horrible thing!" or "Is that even real!" or, humorously, "That is either the ugliest dog I've ever seen or you're on the set of Star Wars." I would answer, "That's my last girlfriend, how dare you!" or "Have you never seen a housecat before? Maybe I shouldn't have moved so close to that nuclear plant." The point is, it got them writing to me, it started a fun conversation—which is the whole point.

Rick, the former army officer, posted a photo of him posing with a fresh hunting kill—a wild boar. A shocking picture like this can be a terrific filter. If someone were opposed to hunting, they probably wouldn't want to date him anyway. And the women that were attracted, were really attracted.

They tell me that the hunting photo was the pattern interrupt that made them write me— nobody else has a picture on there with a picture of a dead pig—it was different.

And because it was different, it worked. Ask yourself—what unusual photos do you have of yourself? No, don't necessarily try to be Rick and head out into your neighborhood with a shotgun. Just start thinking—what's funny? I knew a guy who put up a photo of himself holding the bars of a wheelbarrow full of money. What unusual locations have you visited, or can you? Of course, a photo of you in an exotic locale is a great come-on. It shows you're a world traveler. Stand out from the crowd.

Women want to see that you have resources, yes, but they also want to see that you have *cojones*, that you challenge yourself, that you are a man of the world. A rugged shot of you taking a ski jump or free-climbing never hurt, nor does a shot of you on a Ducati. But that's not the end of the story. You want to add an additional contrast…

Remember, women also value a man who demonstrates that he can *cherish* others. My 14-year-old son, when he was watching the famous "pick up artist", Mystery, giving a talk, all peacocking in yellow goggles and a big furry hat, leaned over to me and whispered, "Dad—it's not that hard. You go the gym, get plastic surgery if you have to—and buy a puppy." Smart kid. The point here—a picture of you with a puppy can't hurt. Or with your kids. Or helping out during a charity event. Or hugging your dear old mom. This humanizes you and makes you less of a threat online. It lets her know you're a real person who cares about real people.

Beyond that, all the common standard rules apply to photos—don't wear sunglasses, it literally makes you look "shady". Smile at the camera! Smiles are the quickest way to feel welcome and attractive. Use good quality photos, not washed out cell-phone pictures that you took at arm's length. If you need to invest in a set of headshots, do it! It's worth every penny. Just go on Craigslist and grab a photographer for $50 to $100 bucks to take a series of shots in good lighting. And as for whether or not to go shirtless, let me quote Rick…

If one more woman tells me the reason she wrote to me was because I was wearing a shirt, I'm gonna go out there and start strangling guys. What's with them? Everyone goes shirtless, but women hate it!

And if you didn't get the message, here's a comment from an attractive woman on the WYP blog…

Guys looking for pay per play on this site are always the ones with [their] shirts off, ladies! It's a huge red flag and a turn-off. I do not want to see love handles with pasty skin! Ugh!

Here are some more essential tips drawn from www.DeepOnlineAttraction.com.

Envision Her

This is one of the most powerful techniques I teach men. Rather than do what every other guy does, and simply list all the wonderful things about you, instead envision her in your profile.

I opened one profile like this, and it ended up getting noticed by the star of ABC's *How To Get The Guy*, and I ended up being "the guy" and dated her for eight months…

You are inspired and inspiring, vivacious and witty, with a great open-hearted laugh. Joy swims around you and everyone notices. You can't help it…

Guess what happened? I got bombarded by women who fit exactly that description! Joyous, happy women.

Just what I wanted. Imagine that! Most men talk about themselves and end up sounding like white noise to women. But put yourself in her place. She's scrolling through profiles and reads scuba diving... blah blah blah... 27 countries... blah blah blah... great friends... walks on beach... and then suddenly she comes smack-dab face-to-face with a precise and admiring description of her! She will write to you and say, "I'm her! I'm the one you're looking for!" Or even, "You have described me better than I could describe myself"—as often happens to me and now to my students.

The key is to be precise in describing what you want so she can recognize herself. In another profile, I began:

I am no cubicle guy and you are no cubicle girl. We are the kinds of people who blaze our own paths, who are restless for discovery and adventure and we don't let other peoples' constricted ideas of how to live fence us in!

That profile lassoed me a whole bevy of adventurous girls, ready to explore the world with me.

So remember, rather than droning on about *you*, think about *her*, and describe her with admiration. And if you can, add images of the two of you out there doing your thing together, a team, Bonnie and Clyde (just don't say "partners in crime"—it's hopelessly cliché at this point and means nothing).

Be a Moving Target

Just as you want to use your photos to create a complex picture of the man you are—friend, athlete, achiever, lover, adventurer, for example—so too you want to make sure that your words don't allow her to dismiss you because you are uni-dimensional.

So, look for ways to counterbalance your primary self-identification. For example, if you see yourself primarily as a "nice guy"... be sure to include something risky, bold, transgressive, bad-boyish. Then she won't see you as too soft.

If you see yourself primarily as an athlete—be sure to include something poetic, sweet, visionary, artistic. Then she won't think you are a *lunk*, or worse, *violent.*

If you see yourself primarily as a geek—be sure to include something masculine, bodily, demonstrating leadership, authoritative, physical. Then she won't see you as *asexual.*

Women are excited by masculine "potential". The key to that word is "potent", or power. By assuring that you don't come off as a one-trick-pony, she will sense that there is something mysterious about you—making you that much more attractive in her eyes.

Be Specific

Instead of saying "I love comedies," say, "My favorite movie this year was _____" and say why. Don't say "I've done some traveling and want to do more," and not even, "I've been to several European cities and some gorgeous Greek islands." Instead, say,

> *Nothing makes me happier than stepping out of a quiet boutique hotel on a Christmas morning in Paris, where the shopkeepers are sweeping the light brush of snow from their sidewalks. The air is filled with the aroma of fresh bread and espresso brewing, everyone seems happy, and you just want to grab someone and kiss them!*

See the difference? Do you see what we did there? Without explicitly saying (like everyone else) that "I've been to Paris," she knows I've been there. Plus we've conjured up a whole sensual scene for her to enter. I gave her the opportunity to feel the chill, to smell the baguettes baking, to feel the romance of the moment—and now she is going to anchor all those sensations to me. Is this kind of subtle touch necessary for your profile? No. Will it skyrocket your attractiveness and draw the best women online writing to you? Yes. You can write about the mountains near your home, the lake where you have a house, the river where you fish. It doesn't have to be Europe. But it does have to wake up her senses and make her want to be with you.

Be Positive

Nobody likes to hear a litany of complaints, especially from someone they don't know. Remember, it's a profile, not a diary. Be upbeat. Say nothing negative about the dating site, about yourself, especially about your ex and nothing negative about women at all. There's enough misery on the news. They don't need it in your profile.

There's another negativity trap: if you have strict guidelines about who you want writing you and who not, avoid saying, "don't write me if you want..." Say instead, "I would love to hear from you if you want...."

Praise Others, Not Yourself

Nobody likes to hear about how great someone is from his or her own mouth, or of their wonderful accomplishments. You're not trying to impress the boss to get the job—you're trying to show potential dates you're fun to hang out with, that you're a good man and you're someone she could admire. This is a relatively easy maneuver and it works like this. What you don't say is...

> *Every Sunday, I head down to Big Brothers and treat all those little kids to my wisdom and knowledge. I think I can safely say that I'm the best mentor they've ever had.*

What you do say, you reveal by praising others rather than yourself...

> *One of the great points of joy and gratification in my life is the faces on the kids down at Big Brothers. I try to get there every Sunday even for a couple of hours. I don't care what happens during the week in my manufacturing firm, nothing beats the laughter of those kids as they discover abilities and knowledge they never had before—and see new possibilities for themselves they never had before.*

The focus is on them—but the glory—100% implied rather than boasted—is clearly on you. These kinds of techniques can mean the difference between attracting a woman who looks like Drew Barrymore versus a woman who looks like Drew Brees.

Don't Embellish, Exaggerate, or Alter Truth

Be a firm stand for truth—and make that stand part of your profile. People lie in their profiles with words and with photos, posting shots taken when they were younger, thinner, or had more head hair. "So far I haven't run into any problems on *WYP*," said one female member. "I was lied to only once, when the guy's picture was at least twenty years old!"

Some degree of lying is inevitable when competing in the online dating culture; people want to be honest, but they also want to be seen in the best possible light. People sometimes describe an idealized version of themselves, subconsciously presenting the self they *want* to be or might even be trying to develop. And sometimes they stretch the truth simply to fit into a wider range of possibilities: for instance, if I'm learning to surf and want to meet other surfers, I might just say I surf, without admitting that yesterday was the first time I managed to stand up, riding a wave.

There's not much point in telling obvious lies about your looks, since your date will see the reality soon enough—and if you've been deceptive, she will be disappointed. Whether you look better in your profile or not, the act of deception itself is a turn-off to most people. Better to be old, fat, and honest than young, gorgeous, and a habitual liar!

Finally, use your truth-telling quality as a benefit, as leverage. Women, for many good reasons, often don't trust the men they see online. In my book, I offer a whole series of ways to induce *trust* so they can get over that hurdle right from the start. One of the most powerful of these ways is to say bluntly, something like...

> *By the way, everything in my profile is true. Integrity is the cornerstone of my life,*

> *my work and all my relationships. If*
> *you're the girl for me, you will be the*
> *same, and your profile will be a standout*
> *of honesty and integrity.*

Once she feels trust, now she will begin to open to you on deeper levels.

For more insight on the art of how to write a profile that intrigues women and puts you in the power position, you can watch the short video posted for you at www.DeepOnlineAttraction.com.

Tips for Women

Women often complain that men's profiles are either too overtly sexual or that they lie about their age. Women lying about their age or weight is common on all dating sites, but is especially resented on WYP because of the honesty the monetary transaction seems to call forth. If you're making a deal, men feel, it should be a square deal, and everything should be on the table, except extra desserts. Says Doug, the serial entrepreneur from NY, now residing in Florida…

> *I hate it when they write 'athletic, slim' and that*
> *they're in marketing—and then it turns out they*
> *are 200 pounds. That's not athletic, and by the*
> *way, 'marketing' is not another word for 'out of*
> *work'. I arrive at my dates ready to really get to*

know a woman. I'm looking for a wife. And when this happened to me, I was thinking of not even paying her. In the future, I won't sit down with anyone who is deceptive. I'm much more careful in the discussion phase now. Either represent yourself accurately or get off the site.

Nowhere is truth and clarity more valued than on WYP. Because that added aspect of cash exchange creates a frame of "fair exchange", honesty is especially valued here. In my own coaching programs, I urge both parties to set a high and honest moral bar from the start. Be very upfront about your values and make the guy live up to the standards *you* set. This is a great way to filter for the kind of man you want right from the start. For example, if you're a truthful person about your life and photos, then go ahead and write...

Honesty and integrity are core values in my life. Everything I've written in my profile is true, and my photos are recent. And I know that the man who will win my heart would do exactly the same. Thank you for being that kind of man.

Not only does a line this attract the *right kind* of man for you—but it also weeds out the liars, who know they have less of a shot for you. Third, it's the best foundation for a truthful relationship, whether it lasts a night or decades. (Writing tip: the "thank you" at the end softens the call, and makes a man feel good about himself for living up to your standards. Now he's in a prime mood to write you.)

There is another key aspect to the profile extract above. Notice that it is written in all positive language, even as it is meant to filter out the liars and scrubs. Many women make the fatal mistake of using negative language directed at the men they don't want in order to chase them away. I call this the "hey, asshole" element in so many women's profiles...

Hey, assholes, don't write me if you're a liar/player/married!

Instead of:

Please be honest/sincerely interested in a relationship/legally single.

The negative approach always backfires, because your negativity, regardless of the subject, also chases away the good men, the men you *do* want. It is better to set the bar high and invite the good men up to your level rather than squash the ones who can't. The more clearly you do that, the more the creepers will be shamed out of writing you in the first place, knowing they can't live up to your standards.

Next, and this is crucial and I can't stress it enough: when it comes to checking off the boxes indicating the type of relationship you are looking for, *don't check all boxes* unless you really have no preference—wifehood or sugar baby or anything in between.

Men repeatedly asked me to convey to you ladies that you specify the one or two boxes that truly reflect your goals. Men on the site generally fall into two distinct camps—those looking for a genuine life partner and those looking for NSA fun. Pick one. If you're not really sure, create two separate profiles with different tones and different pictures and pursue both goals, but pursue them separately.

One member, a warm, avuncular PhD who is also a business owner and outdoor adventurer, says:

> *What I like about WYP is that you can check off what you want, specifically, although so many women don't. They just check off all the boxes! I have to ask them once I open the conversation what they truly are looking for. They seem surprised that they are getting letters from guys they don't want. I'm looking for a real relationship and when they say that they are too, but they have all the boxes checked, they say, "Oh gee, that must be why I'm getting all these weird offers from guys."*

I have written extensively in my comprehensive program for women, www.TheRightManOnline.com, on how to write a profile that attracts *exactly the man you truly want.* Let me review some of the core concepts for you.

First, write from his point of view. He doesn't care, up front, about how much you love your cat or how much you hate your boss. He may care later, once he cares about you, but for now, he wants to know only one thing: will you make his life happier, or not?

So stay focused on all the "victories" that men seek when they first read a profile. In my research, I have discovered that there are thirteen victories than nearly all high-quality men of choice seek. Your job in your profile is to ignite his passion by speaking not only to fulfilling your needs, which is important—but also, equally—to alerting him that meeting you will feel like a beautiful victory! In fact, it should feel like *thirteen* beautiful victories.

Remember, whereas most women's internal monologues sound something like this: "I feel loved... I don't feel loved.... Now I feel loved.... Oh, now I don't feel loved," men's internal voices sound like this: "I am winning! Oh shit! I am losing. Wait! I am winning! Wooo hoooo! Damn, I am losing."

What you want to do is wake up that *"winning"* upswing by alerting him that you are the kind of woman who will put him in the "win" column. That you will be happy, loving, competent, non-argumentative, sexy, wise, and most of all, supportive of his feeling like he is winning with you by having you in his life.

By contrast, you want to avoid any indications that you are bitter, angry, depressed, moody, negative, incompetent, and helpless, argumentative, self-righteous or self-deserving, judgmental, or un-trustable. Those are all ways in which you will make him feel like he has *lost* in life by having you by his side.

Let me show you some examples of how to make him feel like he would be winning by dating you. You should certainly craft these kinds of sentences to be true for you and to express who you are, but here is a start...

How to Evoke the 13 Victories

A woman who is happy is a victory in a man's life. So you want a man reading your profile to feel: "Wow, I will win because she is already happy! I should write to her!" You do this by pouring your joy into your profile. Men are terrified of getting saddled with a Negative Nellie, a buzz-kill, or anyone really who will bring them down. They feel (subconsciously) that their life is hard enough. It feels like a battle out there every day, fighting for status, fighting for recognition, fighting for dignity. Feminine joy is a balm for us, a rejuvenation, a harbor. His heart will leap up when you write...

I love my life! I love my friends, I love the view from my window, my nieces and nephews! I love the aroma of the night-blooming jasmine outside my window and steak broiling on an outdoor terrace as evening falls. And I love holding the strong arm of a trustable man as we head out for a night on the town.

Here's a second example. Men are afraid of getting into a relationship with a woman who will deny him sex—that would not be a victory. Conversely, he will practically lay down his life for an enthusiastic sexual partner. A woman who loves sex is a definite victory for most men.

You can't say, "I love sex!" in your profile (even if you do love it!) or you will get letters from every creep in the world. But you can give him the clues he needs to spark his passion to write you. You want him to feel this when he reads your profile: "I will win because she loves her body and sounds sexually healthy!"

I love my body and feel blessed to be healthy and fit. Yoga is a time to stretch like a cat and feel every inch of myself come alive. I never miss an opportunity to take a long, hot oil bath or find a hot springs along a journey...

I'm breaking into a sweat just writing these words! When he reads something like this, he will suspect that this kind of woman will be a sensual, passionate, enthusiastic lover, which is like hitting the jackpot for most men. His thought will be, "Wow! I'll bet the sex will be fantastic." Watch how much more attention he gives you when driven by this desire. The more you convey that you love your body through dance, fitness, yoga, and all the sensual pleasures, the more alive you remain to pleasure, the more likely the better lover you will be, and the more devoted your man will remain to you.

Another of the 13 Victories is when a man feels a woman will bring joy into his life because she likes men in general, and him specifically. Despite all outward show, a man's inner life can be a pretty arid place. It is a graph, a grid, a series of measurements of his relative winning and losing. You, as the cool, refreshing breeze of the feminine, light us up, inspire us to stop and smell (and buy) the roses, and enjoy life more. Your joy is our elixir. Bring it so he can feel, just by reading your profile, that you love life, and specifically that you love men… for being men. You want him to think, "I will win because she already likes men and will not be angry, negative, or bitter!" Here is an example of how to show you love men…

Can I just say this? I love men! I love you for your strength and steadiness. For the way you raise sons and daughters to be proud and free. For your care and protection and for the way I can rely on you to give good solid judgment in the midst of crises...

By writing in this way, remember, you are also calling forth the specific qualities of the man you hope to meet—and setting the bar where *you* want it!

Another fear men have is that you will try to change him or curtail his highly treasured sense of freedom. Men need to feel that they are making the decisions, even if you have subtly guided him toward the decision. He likes to feel that he is in charge of his life. This is where the womanly arts come into play—your ability to get what you want, what you think is best, by making him think it was his idea! It goes back to Cleopatra and will never change, probably. The key to this one of the 13 Victories, is let him know that you "get" men and won't try to turn him into a doormat or wilted househusband. His inner victory statement will sound like this: "I will win because she has taken the time to learn about men and won't try to change me!"

When looking for a relationship, men worry that women will disallow them from doing the things they love to do, and prevent them from having "guy" time. One of the most painful evocations of this I have seen is in the breakthrough movie *Juno*, where Jennifer Garner's character, in trying to create the "perfect" home, crunches her husband's entire joyful existence—his guitars and memorabilia—into one tiny room of their palatial house. It is a pitiful sight, him there in that crowded prison, dreaming of his freedom, his joy, his happy identity, all but crushed by his well-intentioned wife. Try something like this in your profile:

> *I love men and I love men being men. I want you to keep your hobbies and your sports. I want you to have time with your buddies whenever you need it because I know how important that is for you to recharge and live the life you want. I'm not looking to change you, but to enjoy you, and to share the pleasures and challenges of life together as a team. And teammates let each other play their best game.*

Oh, a line like that is catnip for a strong, directed man.

On the whole, when you write your profile, dazzle him by how amazing it will be for him to be lucky enough to be in a relationship with you. Balance that by being straightforward about your style of life, what you enjoy.

And finally, crucially, don't focus on the characteristics of the man you want, but rather, write in clear terms about the *character* of the man you want.

This is one of the biggest mistakes women make and it costs you years of pain and frustration.

Get this right from the start: specify the character qualities you admire in men, whether it is authenticity, honesty, loyalty, adventurous, kind, protective, or supportive of your dreams.

Who cares if you both like tennis or foreign movies or ice fishing? What is important is the core character of the man you are going to commit your heart to. So why not start out right by being very clear about his character?

Hint: don't "demand" he be this amazing man of character. Just let the reader know that you "admire", "appreciate", and are "turned on" by these particular character qualities.

Doing this alone will utterly change your success.

For more tips on how to write a profile that captures exactly the right man for you, the 13 Victories, and how to call forth the character of the man you want, you can watch the short video posted for you at www.TheRightManOnline.com.

Step 2: The Offer

Tips for Men

How much money should you offer for the first date?

Well, it depends. It depends on how much you have to spread around on multiple dates. It may depend, in part, on the age and attractiveness of the woman you want. If she's in college or her young twenties, $40 or $60 might seem reasonable to her. If she is a woman of stature, who is elegant, who is used to the finer things, who has lived some of her life and gained wisdom and finesse, you'll probably want to bid $100 or above.

Another factor, of course, is location. If you are in New York or Los Angeles, London or Paris, chances are the bids that women will receive are higher than those in Tulsa or Carson City. If you're in New York, for example, the cost of living and the cost of looking good is higher, and if a woman is going to take a taxi, you'd expect to pay a higher rate. Fair is fair.

If you offer too little, you can seem cheap. If you offer way too much, as some men do, bidding $500 or more, women will think one thing: this guy expects me to get in the sack, tonight.

And of course, money represents different things for different people. Some of the women on the site don't care if you bid $50 or $100, as long as you seem like a nice man with real potential. Others may find your physical type or your profile or age unacceptable at any price, and that's fine, too. Move on to the next woman. Not everyone is going to like everyone, no matter what the price.

Rhonda, 29, works in beauty, and has her eyes on the prize. She calls herself a "true beauty" and uses price to filter out men with lesser resources, or at least, less generosity.

If someone winks at me and I suggest an offer— and they come back with 40 dollars, I don't respond. Maybe in a rural district, that's okay. But Atlanta is a major city. 100 dollars isn't a lot of money for the kind of man I want to be with.

Says Sonia, 45, an elegant, charming Argentinean woman currently seeking a true life partner in Miami:

I tend to get offered anywhere between $75-$200 dollars. Really, anything $100 and up is good for me. $75 feels too cheap for a city like this, where there is so much wealth. Though, to tell you the truth, I did take one or two dates at $75 because I liked the guys.

Says Albert, who owns an environmental testing company...

I advise men to get the hang of who is real and who is in this for the money—if you offer a straight $100 and they counter you $500, forget it! She's an escort, or maybe just someone hoping for a quick windfall. In fact, one of the blogs that Brandon (WYP's owner) supplies, warns you straight-up that a crazy-high offer like that is probably an escort or pay-for-play. Me? I have a limit of $200, if she is an extraordinary woman. I offer $100. I think it's fair, it's reasonable, women appreciate it. It pays for her gas in this day and age. If they ask for over $200, I move on. It's a bit of a warning.

As Brandon Wade envisioned it from the start, the offer should reasonably cover the costs of a woman getting ready for, getting to, and making time for the date. If she's asking for $300 or more, she might be using the site primarily to make a little cash on the side, or perhaps she'll ask for some more at dinner to "close the deal". Stay alert to the kind of woman you desire. The important thing is that you have to learn to read between the lines and feel out the person at the other end of the offer.

The question now becomes: if a man makes an offer, should a woman counter-offer? Ultimately, it's a matter of taste. Some people say that if women haggle, it cheapens the process. Says one member, with a sense of exhaustion:

I mean, really, what's $20 dollars? It feels to me a little like she's just squeezing the last juice out of an orange. If you think the guy is decent at $60, is he really that much more appealing at $80?

On the other hand, Wade suggests that if a woman requests, say $120, and your going offer is $100, don't bother haggling her—*if* you really like her. If you are lukewarm about her, you can offer lower.

Truth be told, some people enjoy the give and take of negotiation and some just find it annoying. Says Helene, a surgical nurse in Portland:

I'm not selling wines or merchandise. It's not like a negotiation. I don't like that but I did it a couple of times but I realized it didn't work for me. Some guys love playing the game—they like to negotiate. They seem to get a charge from winning. But these are the guys who generally don't want to go on a date, they just want to play a game. So I don't get involved with that type any more.

At its heart, the whole point of the bid is to compensate a woman for her time and effort, and to give every guy a shot at winning the heart and mind of an attractive woman he might not otherwise have the time or skills to meet. Treat the offer and bid as a simple transaction to ease your way to the first date.

However, money often raises people's hackles and will alert a woman to other issues you may have. It can be a filter as to your attitude to dating, to women, to money and to generosity—and can either support or kill your chances from the start. Sonia tells this story:

My ex was very wealthy so I am used to good things, to being treated well by a man. I am on this site because I want a gentleman of the old school, a man who is a little more upscale. And the thing is, with the offer, you can tell up front if they have a generous nature. Once I specified $200 as my minimum and he came back with $75. He was indignant that I didn't take it! He said, "Look at me, I play polo, look at my pictures in front of my mansion!" I said to myself, you're kidding me! You rejected $200 and you're this multi-millionaire! On your scale, I'm not worth $200? You spend more than that on a bottle of wine. So really, it's not about the money, it's about the attitude. Please don't say, "Hey, baby, check my web site or web page" if you're going to be cheap with me, and expect that your dazzling wealth or success will make up for it. Make a respectful offer. I'm a very attractive woman, and I can meet people every where.

In some ways, money is relative. Just ask any celebrity. When they go to a restaurant, they are pretty much obliged by their fame to leave outsized tips of 50% or even 100% or more. If they have mega-millions in the bank, what's an extra $100 or $400 dollars to them? There is a perception of scale.

At the extreme, I recently heard a story about Charles Barkley who, after terrible delayed service, peeled off his Rolex and handed it to the harried waiter, saying, "Here, you need this more that I do so you can keep track of time better." Stories like this get around, and reflect well on wealthy celebrities. So too, if you are very wealthy, don't scrimp on your offer if you like a woman. Don't flaunt your money lavishly, but make an offer that respects her.

Finally, one member suggests that you use the cash offer as it was meant to be—as a door opener, and nothing more.

> *Guys, be smart. Make a good offer. If you're serious about meeting a potential partner, girlfriend, or wife, then don't make a big show of the money up front. Don't talk big about how you're buying a boat. Listen, there are plenty of wealthy men. If we are on a date with you, we are listening to your heart, not your wallet. Your wallet is only part of what got you here. I won't go on a date if I don't see something sweet or*

endearing about you in your profile. The date is not about money. The date is about "can we create a human connection."

And one final piece of advice from a member in Tennessee...

Men, be truthful. Use current pictures, be respectful. If you want to buy someone for sex, go to Vegas. If you're a toothless old bum, don't go for the Playboy model. This isn't a fantasy site, it's for real. The women I've dated, they're real.

Tips for Women

How much should you ask for as an attractive woman? What should be your minimum? What is insulting and what is too much? These are all questions whose answers are relative to your location, as well as to what you think of the guy. The important thing to remember is that if he proposes an amount and you accept, or if you propose an amount and he accepts, that means you now are in a conversation. The agreement on a price simply unlocks the ability to e-mail each other on the site. You should use that opportunity to either exchange a few e-mails or move to a phone call so you can get a better sense of each other. If you find that he is not what you hoped, or if he is rude or offensive in any way, you can put an end to the dating progression right there, and no cash transaction will ever occur. He will have expended a few dollars on his credits, but that will be the extent of his commitment.

Similarly, if he decides that you are not what he hoped, he can decline to have the date and the arrangement expires. This can happen. Remember, the offer and acceptance only open the conversation. Ideally, both parties enjoy the ensuing e-mail and phone exchanges and a date happens. But neither you, nor he, is obliged to take the accepted offer to the next level of an actual date.

With that caveat, let's review some useful thoughts about how to handle the offer and range of offers.

First of all, it should be obvious to you that a man who offers you $500 is most likely expecting sex. There may be gazillionaires out there who love to lavish money on women for the company, but large amounts should raise your suspicions.

How much should you ask for if he winks at you or if you find his profile appealing? Using the guidelines of what it takes for you to prepare for a date and make all the travel and perhaps babysitter arrangements, in a major city, anywhere between $50-$120 is reasonable. In more rural or outlying areas, $40-80 seems right.

If you are shockingly beautiful, well yes, you can probably command a slightly higher rate, or if you are particularly well-educated, well-cultured or bring "added value" in any other way. L.A. based Rebecca, 35, uses her professional billable time as a guideline:

> *I'm a professional food evaluator—I get $150 an hour to evaluate food. This site suggested that I ask for about two hours of my usual billable hours for a first date and so I do. So, according to the site—two hours of my time would be worth around $300. So that's what I ask for. I'm not trying to make money here, just not lose any. I'm very choosy anyway. I need a very highly educated man, since I'm kind of a nerd myself, so I'm not going to accept most bids, anyway. The right man will recognize a kindred spirit. I have a very detailed profile and he won't balk at my rate.*

When some people first hear of the site, they think it is an open door for women to turn dating into a job, pocketing a couple of hundred dollars a night. But that's not how the members see it. Warns one attractive woman:

> *Ladies—don't treat this site like a job. Be open to offers, it's just a date. But don't lead men on falsely. Don't go out with them if you don't think you'll ever like them or find them at all attractive.*

Go out with men you like—not just because they are paying you. That's not fair to them.

The call to take this site seriously comes from both sides. From the men's camp, the large number of business-owner types who truly want to shortcut the meeting process and get to know some appropriate women, repeatedly ask for the women on the site to take it seriously. Says one father of two who is earnestly looking for his life-mate:

Please remember that it costs us guys money to buy credits to make that first contact with you. If you're not serious, please don't accept the offer. If you're serious enough to accept the proposal, then please follow through and let's us get on the phone and see if we have some chemistry.

This sentiment was repeated by a Midwestern entrepreneur who owns a series of gyms:

The only negative I've seen is that some women accept your offer but then they don't follow through. It costs money to buy the credits. You don't want to spend a bit to open a conversation and then they disappear.

Just because a man has disposable money to pay for a date doesn't mean he wants to waste time and money on the offer and acceptance process with no real results. A millionaire scientist from the San Francisco Bay Area, who has the same complaint, found an elegant solution.

This site is unique because it costs something to open a conversation. I believe women realize that but there is still a percentage of them here that I would call collectors. They will agree to a date or send me a wink. Then they'll accept an offer, but I never hear from them again. That's been the only frustrating part of the site for me. So to solve it, I've added this note to my profile:

Note: I now have some experience on this site and have found that many women reply affirmatively to my offer for a date and then disappear with no follow-up. You may not be aware that it costs men to open a dialogue after you accept, so if you are just into "collecting" offers and have no intention of actually corresponding and going on a date, please do not accept my offer. Just move on. Thanks!

That is an excellent example of employing *positive clarity*, and everyone is encouraged to use his example. He states what he wants without being negative or accusative. He explains himself clearly and remains polite. If everyone behaved like this, online dating would be a more pleasant experience for one and all.

Getting back to the amount offered, if you find it too low to cover your needs, you are free to counter-offer with a higher amount. Some men have no problem with that and may even be turned-on by your self-respect or self-estimation. Others however, may not. It's really a case-by-case feeling.

Paul, for example, is a financial executive in Toronto. He has just finished raising his daughter by himself and wants to find an easy-going partner to ski with, go to movies with, hang out with and enjoy time with. Like many men who seem a bit weary of the battles of life, he says:

> *I don't want to haggle. If I offer $50 and she counters at, say, $100, what am I supposed to say, $75? And then she says $85? What are we doing, then? Is this worth it? I mean, we're just meeting for a drink somewhere. Why introduce all this drama at what should be just a simple moment of an offer and acceptance?*

However...being paid for a date was a new experience for POP. Single, 40, and seeking a husband, while she felt "a little awkward" about the money, she also felt unexpectedly empowered, "like I deserved it."

She seems to be growing more accustomed to it, her confidence building along with her price. "I negotiated both times," she says, "but the first time I was quick to accept any amount. Now I hold out for what I want."

You are free to make a counter-offer. It's entirely up to you, and depends on how you feel about the man. If he doesn't appeal to you all that much, set a high counter-offer to discourage him, to test his seriousness about you in particular or to offset your lukewarm feelings. On the other hand, if you like him, you might want to be more reasonable. If you're looking for someone more like a sugar daddy and a fun NSA experience and want to test him, of course, the sky's the limit.

Again, it's important to clarify that What's Your Price is *not* a sugar daddy/baby website. Sites like SeekingArrangement.com are built specifically for Sugar arrangements. Everyone's welcome to use WYP as well, and the option is there, but don't approach potential dates there with the same expectations as you would on SeekingArrangement.com. Most importantly, as the voices of the men in this book should clearly indicate, do not assume that everyone you meet on WYP is open to a Sugar relationship. Some of them won't even know what you're talking about! The WYP site is geared toward all kinds of relationships, but if the sweetness of a Sugar relationship is more to your taste, SeekingArrangement.com is the place to find it.

Step 3: The Conversation Begins

Once an offer has been made and accepted, the next phase of the process begins. A dialog box is unlocked and the generous and attractive partners can begin to e-mail each other or jump on the phone to start getting to know each other and schedule a date.

Again, there is no obligation to have the date. The offer is the first step, the acceptance of the offer is second—the conversation is the third. If things don't go well during the conversation phase, there is no date.

Maybe you find that your opinions on politics clash. Maybe he is rude or overtly sexual and that's not what she wants. Maybe, unlike on her profile, she is negative and critical. The key is that the agreement for a fixed price stands if you go on the date. If the date never happens, the payment never happens. The man loses some credits in his balance, and can always replenish them at any time. This is the phase where you see if what you think you saw in each other's profiles bears out. So use this phase well and carefully.

Tips for Men

The calculation is simple: you are going to make a real cash investment in a date. If you find in your e-mails and phone conversations that you don't like the woman as you hoped you would, let her know "thank you very much," but you've decided that the date is off. As the generous partner, you only are obliged for the agreed-upon cash payment if you both proceed and show up for the date.

Grant has been a member for over six months, is looking for a wife, and finds that the site is a great shortcut to meeting high quality, highly-attractive women.

> *Sometimes I'll pay for the credits and we talk on the phone and I can tell we aren't going to hit it off, so I won't go forward. For example, there was one girl in San Diego who was too officious. She said she wouldn't meet in the middle and that I had to come down there. The way she said it, it felt as if she were working, as if she just wanted to get the date over with. If felt as if she was treating the date as a job. For money. So I didn't move forward. Okay. No problem. That's part of the game. You have to actually talk to get a sense of who the other person really is.*

The purpose of this phase, the conversation phase, is to get to know each other, just as in any other dating or romance process. Find out more about each other, but avoid personal questions that might compromise her privacy (her last name, her company, her home address). For women, safety online is always paramount and should always be respected. Get a sense for who this woman is. My only caution is to avoid spending too much time on the phone. You do want to leave some room for delicious discovery in person, after all. Too much time on the phone can kill the romance of expectation.

As we have discussed above, many women check all the boxes—from seeking marriage through looking for NSA short-term dating to Sugar relationships. Though it may cost you a few credits to find out, this is a good time to explore what she really wants. Says Alvin, 56:

> *I assume all women on the site are looking for a quality man of means. But it is my task, and ultimately my responsibility at this point, to filter out who is sincerely looking for a relationship and who is looking for money and little more.*

Gary, the attorney by the sunny sea in Los Angeles, lays down the law on filtering:

> *I've dated roughly 15 girls on the site... you'll find everything on the site, so you've got to use your filtering skills. There are definitely girls who need support and want to supplement their income—they really want that 100 dollars. I can enjoy dinner with them but that doesn't really interest me. I'll understand the score by the time dinner is over.*

Some girls are looking for long-term arrangements—like Seeking Arrangement—so I ask them up front, before we meet, "what kind of relationship are you looking for? How many guys do you want to be dating?" If they are not looking for a relationship, the conversation ends there.

Some girls don't know what they want. Their friends think of it as a Match but a little different, a little better. They like the idea of dating of a guy who has a job—tired of their boyfriends who are about to make it with their band. When they don't really know what they want, it's an odd spot to be in. They are usually skeptical. They suspect that we want to turn them into prostitutes. But funny enough, those have turned into best relationships for me. When they see I'm a nice, normal man, they end up wanting to be my girlfriend. I have turned a few of them into short-term girlfriends.

Men, you are not the only ones doing the filtering. Many women are just as tired of the flaking and game-playing that happens on other sites as you are. They ask that you keep things moving forward with efficiency. Said one of the women I interviewed:

This site makes it easier and faster to meet people instead of all the back-and-forth e-mails and drama. A few times I have had to go back and forth in e-mails only because the guy was used to that in the past. Men should just try to line up the meeting instead of trying to get more info to see if he wants to move forward and meet. The hardest part is getting to the meet and that makes this site worth every cent! Men should be happy and willing to pay for less drama!

Finally, just as many men get frustrated when women promise a date and never show up, so too, women sometimes complain that men agree on a price and yet never move things forward to the actual date. They don't enjoy having their time wasted, either. Says Sonia, a beautiful, elegant and well-spoken woman in her forties who has enjoyed the site overall, has these words to offer:

Some guys, they are sick. They only like pictures. All they want to do is see pictures! I have seven photos up, but even after they spend their credits, when they write, they don't set up a date! They just say, "Send me more pictures!" That's so frustrating. Take the risk, baby! If you don't take the risk to meet someone for 100 bucks, you don't take the risk for anything. That may be fine for some people, but that's not my style. I don't want to date men like that. Dawdlers. You take risks in everything in life, and that's how you reap the greatest rewards!

Tips for Women

The Internet is a magical, marvelous environment. It can be a great source of enlightenment and education, such as with Wikipedia or Khan Academy or TED video talks. Or it can be a sewer of anonymous insults and hurt. Just look at any comments thread after a YouTube video, or on political sites, and you will see the worst of humanity, cheek-and-jowl with the best.

Keep your standards high from the start. If a man is going to be disrespectful during your first e-mail exchanges or phone calls, chances are, things aren't going to get much better. Sonia from Miami offers women this advice:

> *Don't let a man be disrespectful just because he pays for a date. First of all comes respect. You can detect their level of respect in the messages that they send. Be alert and pay attention. If he offers his phone number, that's good. It's better that they don't ask mine, because they know I am a woman and I have to feel safety. I respect a man for knowing these kinds of things.*

In other words, use this conversation stage as an extra screening opportunity, just as you would on any other dating site. Rebecca, the bookish 35-year-old from L.A, puts the conversation phase to great use and really drills down with her prospective dates:

Look, there are weirdos on every site and in every bar and club. At least here you have the opportunity to screen. I ask potent, direct questions once a conversation is unlocked: "What is it you hope to find? What are you looking for? Describe in the most detail you can. What experience did you have before, what did you like about that experience?" I get very curious and give men the chance to talk. And you know what? Men tell me wonderful things!

Bill is a sports attorney in New York and he has these suggestions for the women on the site:

Women—you have different challenges. A lot of guys are hoping to use money to create intimacy in the absence of time and effort. My best advice is to ferret that out before you meet—is he really interested in getting to know you or not? Everyone likes sex, let's be frank. But the time and energy that goes into it is a different matter. Women need to be very sincere about who they want to go out with. Try to find guys you actually find attractive and interesting. If we don't click, that would be the end of it! That's the whole point of this site—to cut thought the bullshit. I'm explicit about it. We're supposed to see if we have chemistry—you don't say that when someone hooks you up with a friend. You don't say okay, explicitly, let's see how we get along. Out there off the site, you let that meander over weeks and months and everyone's time gets wasted.

Roger, a small business owner, asks of you the same that women ask of men: to be honest.

Please tell the women on the site to be completely honest. You've found a filter to find exactly the kind of man you're looking for—reasonably successful, willing to put his money where his mouth is. Chances are that he is not a time-waster or a wannabe. All that's missing now is your complete honesty with him.

Some women, especially because cash is part of the first-date equation, want men to be certain to know that sex is not in the cards for that first date. If you feel that a man is coming on too strong, one elegant solution is to arrange to meet for a lunch, rather than a dinner date. But the onus is also on you to be clear about what you want and to follow through. Advises, Gillian, a lithe Texan, age 35:

WYP is a good site if you want a financially viable relationship. But you have to be careful how you define what you're looking for. If you open the door to an intimate encounter for payment, you're becoming a mistress. That's not appropriate if what you want is a real, long-term relationship.

She finds that the straighter she is with men on this site, the more success she has. Everyone is much more up-front, and she finds it refreshing. "I find most matchmaking sites boring," she confesses. "Looking online for matches bores me to death. But I'm having a blast on What's Your Price."

In the best possible scenario, you speak on the phone and you discover that you really like the guy. At this point, the cash has already done its job—it's unlocked the conversation.

One member decided to use WYP to find a successful partner who is serious enough to find a high-quality partner that he will actually pay for the privilege—but she never really liked the idea of actually accepting cash. If a man was to buy her a nice dinner for a first date, that was enough for her. She suggests that if you feel the same way, that you can, like her, say something like this on the phone:

I'm interested in meeting you. I like you. You're the kind of man I admire and you sound like a nice guy. That's what I want. I don't want your money. You don't have to bring cash. I'm just using this site as a screening process. Now, let's go have a nice time.

It's likely that he will be amazed and pleased. He may respect your independence of mind and spirit. He may bring you a gift instead. But remember, he may also be a by-the-books businessman who places integrity first. He may insist that because you accepted the offer, it would be wrong for him not to deliver as promised. He may not want to continue the dating process with you feeling he's welshed on a deal, even if you were the one who initiated the change. In this case, if he still wants to give you the money but you don't want it, stay true to your word and have him donate that money to your favorite charity. If he likes, he can bring the receipt to dinner. This way everyone's happy, everyone is true to their word and principles. And maybe some puppies gets saved.

Nadia not only reads the profiles, but she knows how to read between the lines. Even if men don't declare outright what it is they're looking for, she says, "I can pretty much tell." Of course, she also looks at the pictures, but even those she uses to ferret out a man's character. She rules out anyone who poses half-naked. "I find it a little distasteful," she says, "and if they're showing off their body, you know they probably want sex right away."

During e-mail exchange she tries "to feel them out and see how polite they are. I only go out with guys who are polite." If she doesn't like a man's e-mail behavior it's *hasta luego*, dude!

> *There was this guy who started calling me 'babe' right away. I didn't like that. And, he wanted to go out with me that night! He asked, "Are you free tonight, Babe? I'm down at such-and-such bar." Well, I'm not going out with someone who's sitting around in a bar somewhere being bored and expects me to hop to it!*

Good filtering makes for good dates. Filter well.

Step 4: The Date

"I'm not going to ask a total stranger out in public, but I could on the Internet. The first time I did it, I was trying to figure out how to be discreet. I thought it would be weird if I handed her money. So I handed her a greeting card with a simple 'thank you for meeting me' message inside. Turns out she was as nervous about the interaction as I was, because it was her first date on the site, too. She loved the card, and said, 'That's brilliant!' It seemed obvious to me. On subsequent dates I've been amazed to learn that other guys slide cash across the table..."

—Roger, 47

Now let's talk about the next phase: the actual date. In every respect but one, it is just like any other date. You talk. You exchange stories. You reveal yourselves little by little, chapter by chapter, exchanging surface insights at first, and more profound truths as the night goes on. The one difference is that the generous partner must get the cash that in his possession into the dainty hands of the attractive partner. And he must do this without embarrassing either of them, with care, not breaking the otherwise jovial mood of the date's beginning. In this section, we will explore ways of making this moment not only comfortable, but creative and fun. Ready?

Tips For Men

First things first. A man is only as good as his word, and one way to demonstrate that you are a straight-up guy is to get the cash to her in the first few minutes of the date, in as unobtrusive a way as possible.

Don't make her grab for it. Don't make her reach across the table for an envelope. Don't make her feel cheap for accepting it, or act superior or offended that you have to pay. And above all, don't make her ask for it. Attorney Gary, 56, says the less of a big deal you make of it, the better.

> *I give people money all the time. And I collect it from women, too, for fantasy football. Neither one of us thought that was weird to pass cash over a lunch or dinner table. I realized the weirder I make it, the more uncomfortable it becomes for everybody. I'll hand a girlfriend money over the table to cover expenses from time to time. So it's not a problem. Sometimes straight bills and if I remember before I leave the office, I'll do an envelope.*

In brief: get the cash to her and move on with the date exactly as you would with any other date started on any other dating site. And never make reference to the cash again, even if it's in a joking way. Especially do not refer to the cash with any implication that she owes you anything other than the date itself.

Remember—the cash is merely a door opener and an equalizer. It got you at this table with this beautiful woman.

So, how do you get the cash from your clammy hands into her delicate fingers?

The whole moment might feel awkward at first, but there are two ways to make the transaction flow more smoothly. One is to be extremely discreet and the other is to have fun with it.

The most popular way to pass the cash is to place the bills inside of a greeting card, yes, kind of like your grandmother used to do on your birthday. What a great opportunity to get her laughing with a funny card bought from the store! Or even better, what a great opportunity to show that you have been thinking about her—what she said in her profile or during the conversation stage—by inscribing a thoughtful, unique, and specific comment about how happy you are to be with her. Make reference, if you can, to previous discussions and to what is unique about her.

Feel free to play and have fun with the moment, which is an effective way of minimizing the importance of the money, and of highlighting, instead, your sense of humor.

We laughed a lot on the telephone and, sure enough, we were having such a good time on the date, we never talked about the money. I had to mention it at the end of the date—and he said it was in the car. I was suspicious there for a minute, but he came back in with the funny little doggie-headed purse he had purchased for me. He already knew that I loved my dogs, and inside the purse, there was hard candy, some fun little doodads, and the agreed-upon amount. It was silly and goofy, smart and cute, and I loved the thought he put into it.

Another way of minimizing the money aspect of the date is to include it in a larger, more traditional offering...

The women are blown away when I show up with flowers. I am super discreet about the cash, which I always give them right away to get it over with, and always in a card. Usually I write something like, "I hope today's date results in your smiling for a couple days and thinking what a good time you had."

—Rick, 41

By handling the cash and offering the flowers along with such a sweet, non-presumptuous note, Rick finds, everyone can just relax and get to know each other. He says the most common response to this approach is, "Oh my god, you're the most genuinely sweetest guy I ever met." Not a bad way to kick things off!

Finally, if you know a book she likes (or an interest of hers that can lead you to a book she might find interesting) here is another great idea: buy her the book and place the bills either in the front flap, where it is clearly visible, next to your inscription—another great chance for you to be romantic or funny—or you can slip the bills between the pages of the books, staggered and sticking out a tiny bit each so she can see the full amount she has received in one quick glance. What you don't want to do is tuck the bills tightly between the pages so she has no real idea what's in there without having to pick apart the whole thing. She won't do that and now she'll be wondering all during the date if you put the full amount into the book or if she secretly got stiffed.

The key for men is that you should take the initiative and get the money to her within the first five minutes. This site supports and nourishes straight-shooting, clear-directioned alpha behavior, and the more direct you are, and the more integrity you display in carrying out your word without complaint, the sexier you will appear to most women.

Once you hand her the money, take extra pains not to joke about it, or insinuate sexual expectations. Just move on into normal date behavior. As many men have counseled, some women on this site, especially the new ones, or younger ones, still worry it's an escort site. Bill is a sports attorney in New York:

Here's my advice for men: girls are hyper-aware that all this could feel like sex for money. You don't want the to make them squeamish—you HAVE to give them space. You can't be in a hurry. Brandon puts that warning up—this is not an escort site. So if you have any expectations about the use of that money, if you think it implies commitment to sex—you're done. The girls won't be interested—not the right ones. The less you have expectations, the more they can relax and open up. Treat them with deference and respect and appropriate distance. You didn't pay for intimacy—emotional or physical. You're just paying for face time.

What about women from other cities? Sometimes, you will meet appealing women from hundreds or thousands of miles away and want to fly them out or fly there to meet them. Gary, a wealthy attorney, offers sage advice on this.

I met a girl from Texas. She was brilliant and beautiful. Because of our schedules, we talked for six months before we met. It's such a fun way to build chemistry. She flew herself out to meet me, so I paid for her hotel room. There was no expectation. I didn't ask for a room key. I said if we don't get along, enjoy the rest of your stay, just please don't hit the mini-bar too hard. Happily, we got along great. But if we didn't, that would've been okay, too.

As the first date winds down, and if the date has gone very well, you can give extra money at the end as a token of your delight in her. If you want to avoid the suggestion that you want anything sexual and specific in return, you can add....

You know, you look so beautiful tonight and I really appreciate how you turned yourself out. Plus, I've had more fun talking to you than I have with a woman in a long time, and now that I think about it, $100 was too little. Please let me double that just as a token of my appreciation of what a great time I had. The time with you was worth it, easy.

While you're saying this, slip the money discreetly into her bag or pocket or under a plate. Most women like to be told they're worth a lot.

To make sure she understands that you are not suggesting that the extra money is a procurement for sex, tell her straight. "I know some women might think that I was expecting something extra for this cash, but I am not. I just wanted you to know how highly I valued tonight, and I look forward to our next date."

Let's talk for a second about where to go on your date. Dinner is the most common choice. Lunch is a nice, innocent way to meet, although the romance is going to be a bit more distant. If you can get a booth, get one, as it creates more intimacy. If you can get a table with a romantic view of a river, landscape, cityscape or garden—all the better. Dinner cruise? That's golden. And if you can sit kitty-corner to her, that's the best, so you can avoid that forced opposition-across-the-table feeling. Environment is half the game.

If you can come up with a fun activity to complement dinner, it's preferable. If you can stop in at an art opening or catch some jazz and a cocktail first, walk along a beach or arcade—fantastic. Its fun to eat where you can walk afterward and watch street-performers. It helps bond you. To get the most potent bonding experience, hop on a roller coaster or stand atop a cliff. Research shows that the hormones released during a fear moment is almost exactly the same as those when you fall in love, which is why men have intuitively known that bringing their high school date to a scary movie is a good move.

Some more information on what women like...

Two questions were recently posed on the WYP site asking women what turns them on or off about a man on a first date.

Here's what turns them on—

- a good listener□
- a gentleman who does things like open doors for me.
- respects boundaries and isn't pushy
- honesty

and here's what turns them off—

- a disheveled appearance
- being too touchy-feely
- being impolite or rude to service people, such as waiters
- asks invasive questions, especially of a sexual nature, even when I say I don't want to talk about something.

Tips For Women

The first set of tips for women on WYP are the universal tips I always share for online dating:

1. Do not give out your full name or place of work or address over the phone before meeting a man. Many women will not do any of these until a second or third date, or beyond. Safety is first.

2. Never lend money to a newly-met man—and especially never send money electronically NO MATTER WHAT. I have seen too many trusting women send money overseas or across state lines, never to see it again.

3. Always agree to meet for a date in a well-lit, well-trafficked public area. Do not meet in parks, isolated spots, or his place. Safety. Safety. Safety. As one member who received several winks and has gone on dates in the $120 range cautions...

I like the site. I don't think the payment comes with strings attached—no more than any other first date. It all depends on how you go about it. If you say, "Hey, let's meet in a hotel," yeah, that's about sex. If you say, "Let's go to dinner" and make the boundaries clear, then it's fine. My date was a gentleman about it. He put the money in a card. Even though we didn't go out again, I felt like I didn't lose anything, because of the money.

4. See if you can get his name and Google him or look him up on Facebook. Sometimes you will discover he is married—sometimes, that he is even better than you expected.

5. Use a SEPARATE DATING E-MAIL ACCOUNT that does not use your name or your work or have any clue to your personal life. It's harder for men

to track you if you decide to cut off contact. It's easy to set up a new account on Gmail or any service.

6. For the first date, let your family or a friend know where you are and the phone number and identity of the man you're meeting. I have been told about an app called Datetracker Alert. It works like this: before going on that first date with the guy you met online, you enter the date and set up a check-in time. If for some reason you don't check in as scheduled, an alert will be either e-mailed or texted to your emergency contact. It can also send your cell phone GPS location to help locate you. This provides an extra layer of security for you and should help set your mind at ease when meeting someone for the first time.

7. Some women use separate phone lines for their online dating phone to keep their privacy intact. You can easily do this through Google Voice or through buying a cheap, throwaway mobile phone specifically for your online dating life

8. Don't drink too much or leave your drink unattended. Staying alert is obviously key—and although it is criminal and extremely rare—you want to assure that nothing is dropped into your drink.

9. Don't let him pick you up for a first date or let him know where you live or work.

More than half of all singles use online dating in one form or another. But that does not mean you shouldn't take thorough precautions to protect your safety. The fact is you are going out with a stranger, whom you know only from an online profile, and letting them into your life.

Caution doesn't end after the first meeting. How safe you feel with someone is highly individualized. Avoid making up universal rules such as, "If he hasn't done anything weird by the third date, I'll let him drive me out of town." You might know in your bones a person is trustworthy on the first date—or you might not know until the tenth. You must evaluate the people you date on a case-by-case basis and always err on the side of caution.

I can attest, as a male dater, that I respect a woman more who knows how to guard her privacy in the beginning and who takes the time to vet me before I learn her address, place of work, or even last name. It makes me feel that this is a smart, trustable woman, someone who I would like to have on my side. In fact, in my dating guidebook for men, I specifically suggest that no matter which site they use, they write something like the following to a woman:

I realize that online dating can be a big unknown for women, and so while I like to be chivalrous and call you first, I understand that many women don't like to give out their phone numbers to someone who is still a relative stranger. So if you would like to call me first, here is my number. XXX XXX XXXX. Either way, I look forward to speaking with you and learning more about each other.

Ladies, play this site straight, and use it as its intended. Keep your antennae up for strange behavior. One attractive member says that one man she met for a first date said he'd rather give her tickets for a weekend in Hawaii than give her cash. Another woman responded bluntly: "Having a guy offer tickets to Hawaii instead of cash is crazy! That is how you end up dead." Smart woman. Have fun. But be cautious. Bill, the New York attorney, adds…

Women I've dated from WYP have two complaints. First that sometimes guys post old photos. Second, some guys trying to sucker them into things—guys will take girls shopping on a first date and during the process they will slip in a statement suggesting that they will have sex later. And when the girl protests that's not what she thought was going on, the guys will just put the selected shit down and leave. The worst case is the guy who got all these dresses into a woman's hands before he told her his plan. So she felt a sense of reciprocity—which is—excuse me, but I am lawyer after all—a perceived possessory interest in something. To give it up is much more difficult. But most of the women said they met nice guys and have gained some long-term friendships."

Guys like Bill wholly understand a woman's need to feel safe, and in my opinion, a guy like him should be treasured. He tells this story...

I even told one girl who seemed a bit nervous about a first date to bring a friend. If you're worried about it, we'll all sit around and see how we get along. Pick a place YOU feel comfortable. I'll even say, pick somewhere you feel you can run quickly from if you need to. I joke with them at the date. I always ask if they've received the emergency phone or text message yet so they can say Grandma died, giving them a reason to leave. I give a woman all the outs.

Beyond that, you set the pace when it comes to respect. There are two categories of men on the site.

There is a contingent looking for pay-for-play—for NSA or "mutually beneficial" Sugar relationship, rather than a deep soul connection or partner. If you have purposely attracted these men by specifying NSA and "mutually beneficial" relationships on your profile, then you must be able to articulate exactly what you want when you meet for your first date. Get acquainted, feel him out, see if there is lightness and chemistry.

If there isn't, of course you are perfectly free to leave after the first date with a "thank you", an acknowledgment that the transaction is over (you can also do this by phone or e-mail if you feel he will take the news hard or if you want to avoid conflict) and that's that. The key is to put safety first and to keep your dignity and self-respect and resolve crystal-clear and always forefront.

The second category of men is those genuinely looking to find a partner and who are willing to put down cash to see if you have chemistry together. If you have been clear in your profile that you are not looking for a sugar daddy or NSA casual relationship, clarity will be served and you will both be on the same page. Some women find it's helpful to get a man to relax during the first date by saying something like...

I know a lot of men are nervous about the first date. They are wondering if there will be sex at the end of it. So let me tell you what I think works best. Let's just agree now that sex is off the table tonight. Now we can both relax and just enjoy getting to know each other without all that pressure. If everything goes well, we have our whole future together.

Says one member, "I have never had trouble with the dates from WYP. The men on the site treat me with respect because I carry myself with respect."

As for handling the cash exchange moment, here is what I consider the most gracious way to bring about the transaction if the generous partner doesn't offer the money right away...

Exchange the normal niceties, how great you look, how awful traffic was, what a great ambiance this restaurant has. Then before five minutes have elapsed, feel free to say something like...

Thank you so much for agreeing to meet me here. 100 dollars was such a gracious offer and I want you to know I'm happy to be here. You seem very sweet/nice/handsome. It will truly help me out and it shows me that you are serious about getting to know me—unlike other men.

Then...shut up! Any good negotiator knows you put your best out there and then clam up and let the other guy speak next. At this point, if he has forgotten, or if the money transaction feels awkward for him (as it does for plenty of first-time users), this eases him reaching into his pocket, remembering the card, and sliding it across the table.

Now let me take a moment and break down the layered psychology of the statement above...

1. "Thank you so much for agreeing to meet me here..."

With this opening statement, you're already thanking him for "keeping his agreement". This not only sets up you are acknowledging and appreciating him as an "agreement keeper" but you are opening with social grace.

2. "100 dollars was such a gracious offer..."

Now you subtly (sort of) remind him of the exact amount so that there is no vagueness about what you agreed upon. There rarely is, but saying the number out loud makes it more real and present. I like the word "gracious" because it feels kind and cultured and polite. If you say "was such a generous offer", it devalues you. You're worth it! If the offer was only 20 or 40 dollars, and he's not rich or you're in a more rural or economically depressed area, you can use another word. You can say...

40 dollars was a nice offer. I do appreciate that dating can get expensive for a man.

3: "...and I want you to know I'm happy to be here."

This little statement helps him relax. Remember, he may find passing money over the table as awkward as you may feel receiving it at first, so this lets him know that this isn't just a cold, financial exchange. The money is just part of the bigger picture, and big picture is now framed by your happy acceptance of him.

Furthermore, you should realize that because you have accepted compensation for the date, he might be doubting his attractiveness in your eyes, since he "bought" the date. While many of the men on this site seem to be extraordinarily confident men who come because of the business-like, no-nonsense aspect of it, many will be shy "nerds" in the broadest sense—and they might doubt you like them. They might suspect you just needed the 75 bucks or whatever.

Reassure them that this isn't true—that you are happy to be there with them and see if there is chemistry.

4: "You seem very sweet/nice/handsome."

Say something specific and unique to HIM so that your happiness for being here has meat on the bones. This lets him know that you mean it, that you already "see" the good qualities in him, well beyond the cash.

5: "...it will truly help me out"

If it is true that the cash makes it easier for you to prepare for a date or even handle your home bills, acknowledge that, if you wish. It reduces the mercenary sheen that may color the moment. In other words, some men may suspect that some women just date for dollars every night, collecting 80 bucks here and 150 bucks there and have no interest in the men they are dating. While this is possible, it would be a very rare instance! Nevertheless, it puts him more at ease and subtly ignites his "hero" instinct. And all but the most venal of guys want to be a hero for women.

6: "...and it shows me that you are serious about getting to know me"

Hammer-lock! This little statement brings him back to the fact that this is serious business, that he's not a flake, that there is a goal to be accomplished tonight. It also raises your status by reminding him that he has purchased the opportunity to get to know you—and by saying this you are saying that there is enough in you to merit the bought date. It also sets him straight that this isn't about sex, but about him getting to know you, and seeing if there is any chemistry.

7: "—unlike other men."

Ahhh, flattery. Every man wants to feel special, unique and most important, "above" other men. They want to feel different and better, especially in women's eyes. So by saying this, you not only flatter him, but you are saying, more or less, *"Okay, buster, hand it over, because if you don't, you are no better than any average schmuck."*

If he forgets or neglects to hand cash over in the first few minutes, take this structure and let him know that NOW is the time to make the transaction. Put the above in your words, whatever feels comfortable for you as well as for him.

I offer you the above subtle psychology because men, too, don't want the harshness of a cold transaction right up front. Kevin is a marketing director in Atlanta:

Women don't really ask for the money. The thing is, it makes more sense to do it in the beginning, but that's also the time that the attention should be on each other. I think I would be put off if we focused on money first thing at sitting down. It should come after we say hello and settle into our seats and exchange a few pleasantries. It's part of the date, and shouldn't be the opening shot right out of the gate. Otherwise, it's like, "Whoa, hold on, Nelly!"

As you will see in the "men's tips" section, I suggest that men enclose the cash in a greeting card or gift book. Nobody likes to see cash pushed across a table. This isn't Vegas or a bookie joint. A greeting card gives him a chance so say something sweet or funny, and a book gives him a chance to show that he has taken the time to think about you, what you might enjoy reading.

Either way, just say "thank you," discreetly check the amount so fair's fair, slip it away, and put your attention wholly and emphatically on *him*. This makes the money part of date go away quicker, and now you can both relax into focusing on getting to know each other.

Sometimes, men will give half up front and half at then end of dinner. In a man's mind, this may allay his fear that a woman will take the money, get up, go to the bathroom and vanish. Although this has never happened, to our knowledge, some guys imagine the worst.

Sometimes men will offer the money at the end of the date, although we encourage the opposite. Nevertheless, it can remove the anxiety of the cash exchange and as one woman member commented:

> *I like it at the end of dinner, when he said give me a hug and kiss on the cheek—and he slipped me cash into my pocket.*

As noted above, if the date has gone exceedingly well, men will sometimes give extra money at the end as a token of their pleasure at meeting you. If he is clear that he is not expecting sex or anything, but it is a pure acknowledgment, then accept it graciously and make no further mention of it ever again.

In Conclusion

Be smart. Filter well. Know what you are worth. Put safety and respect first. And have fun! Know that Brandon Wade and his team will ban you from the site if you are explicitly an escort or treat your date like one. His team, in fact, has several policies in place to assure members are being truthful and keeping their commitments. He has a team that individually approves every profile to prevent blatant attempts to use the site to procure sex, as well as every photo, to assure they conform to the company's decency standards. The rules are clear: no nudity, no explicit sexual offers, and Wade's team is alert for fraud on all levels.

Men—use contemporary photos and have yourself a follow-up plan if the date goes well. Offer her a few options at the end of your successful date:

Hey, you know, there's this concert next Saturday. I think you'll really enjoy it...

Or...

There's this exhibit on Etruscan Vases at the Met—I've been wanting to go. How about next Sunday and we'll grab lunch at the Bistro?

The point is—a man with a plan is sexy. Vagueness just isn't.

A note to attractive members—if a generous member and you agree on a price for the date and he doesn't pay up—please report him to WYP. You also have the right to take him to small claims court and the agreement is a binding agreement. On the other hand, there have been cases where the generous party refuses to pay because the attractive party used false photos or false representation. In these cases, the WYP team will determine who is in the right, and appropriate action will be taken. CEO, Brandon Wade has said,

> *It's important for everyone to know that we do have rules. If you show up and the person is not who they look like, you have the option to walk away. If you haven't started the date, you're not obligated to pay...*
>
> *Sometimes a woman will complain about a man. This one woman was very upset that he didn't pay. But when I asked, she said she was uncomfortable about asking him. In that case, there is little I can do. If she did ask and he refused to keep his commitment, I will usually take his profile off the site.*

WYP takes extra precautions to keep truth up-front-and-center throughout the site. If you decide to become a member, watch the instructional videos and read the FAQ page. Infringements are taken seriously. Cautions Wade:

> *After one infringement, a member will get a warning from my team. After a second, the account is put on suspension, and we tell them why. They can apply to reconsider, and that will involve a verbal or written commitment to apply again...*

Sometimes, he has discovered, people out there are working out their own problems and hostilities, through dating, so the WYP team always double-checks complaint stories...

> *There was one man who was complaining about a woman on the site he claimed was rude. "Well, I checked the e-mail exchange between them—all exchanges are archived—and I saw that he was aggressively asking for sex for money. So I suspended him.*

And above all, stay polite. One unexpected result of the insertion of money exchange into the dating process, according to one busy Harvard lawyer, is that it "frees" the man from all the messiness of the post-date letdown.

I love this approach! I have more control on this site. I don't feel as if there is an obligation. On other sites, women get upset if I don't follow up after a nice date, or call her. They write me mean letters! Here, there's less of an obligation because there is already a fair exchange on the date. Time for money. If the chemistry isn't there, the deal is done. No apologies, no crying.

You might imagine that a dating site with tens of thousands of members would be automated and impersonal. But CEO Brandon Wade is curiously enthusiastic to "get his hands dirty" and stay close to the experience of everyone involved. I find it a wonderful transformation, because he was once such a social outcast, and now he is a deeply present figure both for members and in the media. As he has written,

I enjoy it! It's a way for me to communicate with people who can share their pain, joy, or success stories with me. It allows me to improve the services I'm providing. Of course, by putting myself out there on TV and radio, I get a lot of hate mail—from feminist groups, that I'm selling "attractive" and I'm making things superficial. Or they think I'm promoting immorality.

Nevertheless, Wade reviews e-mails sent to him, keeps a blog running for members where he comments on posts and counsels some people directly. He laughs, remembering how awkward he a was as a young man...

> *I never saw this in my future but I've counseled a lot of people. People say they've been on the site for a year but not finding the right person. That's why I want to have more dating training for both men and women. Or if they meet someone bad, I tell them to use common sense. What is wrong with setting a higher standard? I teach them to set a goal, to set goals and expectations and manage them rationally. To have a plan.*

In a world of impersonal Internet services and detached CEOs, Brandon Wade stands out as a passionately, even boyishly enthusiastic participant in his customers' experience. He knows he is doing something experimental, and like the engineer he a was trained to be, he is dedicated to tinkering with his creation...

> *What's Your Price is, as I've pointed out, experimental, something that's never been tried before. I'm learning how to improve operations as much as users are learning to improve their experiences. Anyone who's had any problems, I*

ask them, please, always let me know about them. It's going to take some refining and tweaking on both sides, but I'm confident that eventually What's Your Price is going to help a lot of people find what they're looking for, whether it's a succession of steady dating partners, or a lifelong soul mate.

In many ways, this is the dedication not only of a highly professional business mind, but the devotion of someone who has been through dating hell and back. The way I see it, between the lines of every profile on What's Your Price, listening in the background of every conversation starting, sitting like a benevolent spirit at the table of every first date created on the site, is that seventeen-year-old boy in Singapore, so adept at school, yet tripping and falling on his face in front of the one girl his heart yearned for, wondering if he would ever feel the kiss of another's lips, or know the company of a loving partner.

I wish this site existed when I was young! The act of paying a date through an online system like WYP would have removed my fear of asking directly for a date. Not only would I have been able to go out with the kind of woman I was too scared to approach face to face, it also would have given me an opportunity to learn about women! I had nowhere to even talk to them. I believe WYP would have helped me overcome some of my awkwardness, and given me a jump-start on becoming the man I wanted to be. The loneliness and pain of my experience, however, did give me something of value I wouldn't trade for the world: empathy. I feel for all the shy young men and women, or for anyone who has problems, for whatever reason—poverty, disability, real or imagined unattractiveness— asking someone for a date or finding someone who'll ask them for a date. I've come to realize that I wasn't the only person with those dating issues. I wasn't the only one in pain. And I know that the suffering still goes on. Almost everyone wants to find and connect with one special person. And if they find it through WYP, that makes me feel like I've done something great in the world.

THE END

EPILOGUE

One of the happiest surprises in interviewing so many members of What's Your Price was learning how articulate and determined both men and women were to avoid the mistakes of other dating sites. Almost to a one, they expressed a genuine desire to find dates who were interested in meeting them, to avoid the meat-market mentality and the hit-or-miss nature of so many other venues.

Dating, in my view—and in Brandon Wade's—is an unparalleled opportunity to grow, to learn, to deepen not only your empathy for others but also your more general wisdom, so that you can live a happier, more fulfilled life.

Unlike your workaday world, dating is your realm to create as you see fit. It is your playground, your workshop, your living artwork to design according to your tastes and ambitions. Whether you are attractive or generous (or both), male or female, gay or straight, I am a passionate believer that you have the right to create the intimate life with others that you want, as long as you do it truthfully and with respect for your partners.

As Brandon's story makes clear, the world does not prepare either men or women well with expertise in dating, attraction, better, more connected sex, or relationships. Most of us fumble along as best we can until we pick up information that makes sense. We listen to older brothers and sisters. We watch movies for clues. We Google for random information, and ever so slowly, if we pay attention and put to use what we learn, we learn to be better daters, better in bed, and better in long-term relationships.

But some of you want to accelerate your success. Some of you are tired of being frustrated with not finding exactly the types of partners you seek. Some of you have been in long relationships and are rusty and need a refresher course on what is the best way to date successfully, what works and what doesn't work any more.

It is for these reasons that, through the auspices of WYP, Brandon Wade and I will be creating a special three-month coaching program to help you hone your dating skills and goals, sharpen and improve your communications, and identify and attract EXACTLY the kind of partner you most desire.

Most people spend endless, frustrating years searching the horizon for that "perfect" partner. But the truth is that you only find your perfect partner when you take the time and effort to become the perfect partner for that person once they arrive on the scene. If you don't take the time to sharpen your skill sets and your communications—as we will offer in this coaching program—you and that person will not connect in the ways you hope.

In the soon to be launched What's Your Price Guaranteed Girlfriend and Guaranteed Boyfriend Programs, you, along with the other men and women in this inner circle, will learn every tool, technique, and idea you need to attract the highest quality of partner.

You will learn how to not only trigger attraction in the first moments, but you will also learn how to inspire devotion that can last as long as you desire.

There will be Three Stages to this program...

The first will be your inner preparation to meet and inspire an extraordinary, evolved partner by mastering the subtleties of masculine-feminine desires and chemistry, by freeing yourself of any habits of negative self-talk or self-sabotaging behavior, and by understanding secrets of gender psychology so you don't make the mistakes that so many men and women tragically make.

The second will be a comprehensive guide to how to meet, intrigue, filter, and delight the most desirable and extraordinary intimate partner you can imagine, both online and socially.

And in the third stage, we will have surveyed and boiled down the best of the best relationship tools and techniques so that you can consciously create a relationship with clarity and open communication from the start, maturely navigate any conflicts that arise so that you both feel safe, supported, and better than when the conflict arose in the first place (deepening your connection instead of breaking it), and finally, how to turn your sexual and erotic connection into something that not only blows both of your minds, but also opens you both up to whole new depths of intimacy, both the light and the dark, the likes of which most people will never know.

Think of this course as your PhD in Dating, Sex, and Relationships, because that is how it has been designed. With it, you will be trained and prepared to meet and inspire the type of lover you have always dreamed of.

This will be a limited program for those who are genuinely serious about being great at dating and relationships. It will includes a twelve-week video curriculum and a weekly group coaching call to answer any and all questions you may have. Because of the personal touch and advanced nature of the material, spots will be limited. Once the program is launched in 2013, it will be available through WhatsYourPrice.com so please check the website regularly.

Whether or not you attend, both Brandon and I wish you success and happiness in your journey.

I hope you enjoyed this book, that you learned a lot and are inspired to get out there and date happily, honestly, and with a great spirit of adventure and fun. I welcome your comments and questions at the e-mail below.

To Your Best Life,
Adam Gilad
May, 2012

Adam@AdamGilad.com

P.S. If you want to learn more, there are videos for men and women that will tell you more.

For men, please visit
     www.DeepOnlineAttraction.com

For women, please visit
     www.TheRightManOnline.com

For inquiries regarding WhatsYourPrice.com or Brandon Wade, please e-mail:

Book@WhatsYourPrice.com

Made in the USA
Las Vegas, NV
25 August 2021